ABC
of
Poultry Raising
A COMPLETE GUIDE FOR
THE BEGINNER OR EXPERT

by J.H. Florea

SECOND REVISED EDITION

DOVER PUBLICATIONS, INC.
NEW YORK

Published in Canada by General Publishing Company, Ltd., 30 Lesmill Road, Don Mills, Toronto, Ontario.

ABC of Poultry Raising, first published by Greenberg Publisher in 1944, was reprinted by Dover Publications, Inc., in 1975. This second, revised edition of the work was first published by Dover Publications, Inc., in 1977.

International Standard Book Number: 0-486-23201-8
Library of Congress Catalog Card Number: 76-15692

Manufactured in the United States of America
Dover Publications, Inc.
180 Varick Street
New York, N.Y. 10014

Contents

Preface

This book is an attempt to explain in the simplest possible terms the basic information needed to raise chickens successfully. It is just as suitable for the general farmer with a small flock as for the backyarder in town.

Although written on the assumption that the reader has little or no knowledge of poultry when he buys this book, the information in it is sound, up-to-date, and sufficiently complete to enable any person to secure profit, as well as pleasure, from his flock.

After all, the principles of sound poultry raising do not change with the size of flock. Exactly the same principles required in rearing 25 chicks in the basement are required for rearing 25,000 on a commercial poultry farm. The only difference is in the equipment used and in the details of applying the principles outlined.

This, frankly, is not a book for the large-scale poultryman. It is suitable for the person who has an interest in poultry, but who must "start from scratch" in his search for knowledge, while the backyarder or farmer who already has a small flock will find that it presents explicit information which will help him make his small flock profitable, and, if he wishes to do so, build it into a larger enterprise. The "what to do" is emphasized rather than the technical reasons for following specific practices or the proof of their value as found in college research reports and similar sources.

Once these basic practices have been mastered, it is a simple matter to keep up to date through current poultry and farm magazines, bulletins issued by colleges and commercial organizations, and the more technical books.

The interest in small flocks may fluctuate with economic circumstances but it never really disappears. There was tremendous interest during World War II (when the first edition of this book was published) because of the ease with which a few chickens could supplement rationed meat supplies. In later years there has developed the strong "back-to-the-land" movement. Many people want the satisfactions and security which a small plot of ground with chickens and a garden provide. The information in this book is just as applicable in one period as in another.

Many far-sighted people have urged greater decentralization of industry, permitting the average industrial employee to have a country home with a city wage. Not only does the country provide an ideal environment for a family, but, as Henry Ford once pointed out, "A man who has one foot in industry and the other on the soil is about as secure as he can be in this world."

Since practically every person who attempts to get one or both feet on the soil depends upon chickens for a part of his living, it is our hope that this book will help to make such an attempt more certain of success.

As in all industries, the methods and tools used in poultry keeping undergo constant change and improvement. The basic requirements, however, change very little. So the same principles of good management which were emphasized in the first edition of *ABC of Poultry Raising* continue to be stressed in this latest revision. It is in the details of operation that most of the revision has been made. Equally important, the reader is directed to dependable sources of information on those practices likely to change most rapidly. Once the fundamental principles of poultry raising are understood, there is constant need to keep up to date through magazines, suppliers, and your state agricultural college extension service.

Grateful acknowledgment is made of the helpful suggestions made by others working with me on the *Poultry Tribune* staff, particularly O. A. Hanke, Milton Dunk, Mahlon Sweet, and M. C. Small, and

Bentley Wilson, all of whom critically read major portions of the manuscript and helped in other ways with its preparation.

Special acknowledgment also is made for permission to use so liberally of photos from the *Poultry Tribune* files.

The chapter on fitting and showing poultry is by courtesy of John L. Skinner, poultry extension specialist, University of Wisconsin. Licensed by the American Poultry Association as a poultry judge, he has taken an active part in promoting poultry shows. He believes strongly in the values of this hobby phase of poultry keeping.

I

Introduction

More people raise chickens than keep any other food-producing animal. This is a strong statement, but a little reflection on the number of small flocks which are kept on farms and suburban homesteads makes it easy to believe. More than one-fifth of the farmers in the United States have a flock of chickens, and while the number of nonfarm flocks has never been counted, it surely would be no exaggeration to say that they run into the hundreds of thousands or even millions.

Why should chickens hold such fascination for both farm and city folks? Out of some 40 years of intimate studying, observing, and working with chickens, it seems to me there is only one simple answer—they provide more pleasure and profit (in either food or dollars) for the work and investment required than any other animals.

The pleasure to be derived from a flock of chickens is not easy to put into words, for it means different things to different people. Basically, I think it is found in the love of taking care of something alive, something which responds quickly to good care, something which has life and individuality, and which takes us back to the soil without the necessity for large acreage or expensive equipment. For not many of us in the United States are yet so far removed from the farm that we have lost that desire to "have one foot on the soil."

And the pleasure to be derived from chickens is no respecter of persons. It may seem easy to comprehend why the factory worker may like to compensate for the monotony of routine work with inanimate things by caring for a flock of chickens at home. But did you know that many of our large industrialists get personal delight out of a flock of chickens, although it may be nominally the project of a young son or daughter? Perhaps not many people know that many of the stars in the entertainment world have had large flocks of poultry on their ranches and are proud of their success with chickens. On the entry lists of poultry shows throughout the country will be found names of people of wealth and social prestige who get delight from pitting the results of their poultry breeding skill against that of hundreds of others. Surprisingly enough, one of the most coveted poultry show awards was put up by one of New York's best known playboys.

Chickens have no peer as a project for boys and girls, and on many a farm I have visited, the owner has taken me to a small poultry house and opened the door with the proud comment, "This is the boy's (or girl's) 4-H Club project." This is truer still in town. A small flock of bantams or large fowl provides work of fascinating interest for boys and girls who need to deal with live things. Such a flock establishes habits of regularity, gives experience in buying and selling, keeping records, and other business activities. Then, too, the fact that they will more than pay their way takes them out of the class of expensive hobbies.

In one family of my close acquaintance, the "poultryman" is a six-year-old boy who has each of his hens named, and who takes great delight in reviewing their good and bad points for visitors who show an interest in them.

Of course, there are disappointments too. Sometimes the chickens die, or egg prices are too low to show a profit. But isn't that a part of life too?

Lest you think I am overemphasizing the benefits of the small flock, let me add that most successful large poultry farms today have grown from a small flock, kept either as a backyard project in town or as a few hens on the farm originally raised to provide eggs and "pin money" for the family. Examples are endless. There was the northern Indiana poultryman who moved to a farm and started with poultry after he had lost a good job in Chicago. He was nearing 50 when he made the move to a new way of life, but he gave an excellent demonstration that it is not difficult to succeed with poultry if one is willing to learn the desirable practices, then apply them. Not only was he healthy and happy with his flock, but he was better off financially. He commented, "My annual income from chickens is equal to twice that much in Chicago."

There were the two Ohio poultrymen, one a war veteran and the other a college graduate in engineering. Each began with a small flock of chickens and found it was profitable enough to justify expansion into full-time operation. And the New York immigrant and his wife who soon wearied of the "fast city life" and bought a seven-acre farm with 1,500 layers, two cows, and a pig. Growth didn't come easy, but they eventually became successful egg producers and marketers on a very large scale.

On many of the fine farms of the Midwest, a flock of poultry kept the farm going through the depression years. Time after time, accurate records have shown a properly managed flock of chickens to be the best-paying enterprise on the farm.

One of the largest and best-known poultry farms in the United States and one which has influenced the practices of more poultry raisers than almost any other one was built up by a rural schoolteacher who saw the possibilities in poultry.

One of New England's best-known poultrymen began with a backyard flock while he was working in industry. With no other experience he moved to a farm and has since built up his poultry enterprise to approximately 25,000 birds.

Several of our best-known breeders and winners in egg-laying contests were owners and managers of fair-sized manufacturing businesses until well along toward middle life when their interest in poultry took over first place.

Early in life I learned the importance of a good flock of poultry on a general farm. At marriage, my parents began farming with very little capital. My mother, like most farm women, had a small flock of chickens. Unlike most of their neighbors, however, they kept detailed records on their farm enterprise. From those records, they discovered that the chickens were surprisingly profitable. The number was expanded to several hundred, a large flock for that day, and with brief interruptions which were no fault of the chickens, poultry thereafter continued as their main source of income.

A parallel example is that found on a recent visit to an outstanding Illinois farm where dairy cows and hogs had been the principal livestock on the farm until the son and his wife, both agricultural college graduates, returned to the farm and began keeping careful records. Chickens had been ignored to the point where they didn't produce even enough eggs for the family use. A small flock was established, given good care, and the records soon showed its true worth.

Figures may be dull, but if you are interested in chickens, you ought to know just how important they are in the agricultural economy of this country.

Over the years, farm poultry and egg production has accounted for approximately 10 to 12 percent of the total United States gross farm income. The gross income from all poultry products amounts to approximately six billion dollars a year. This allows nothing for the large, but untabulated, production of nonfarm flocks.

Perhaps a few other figures on the size of the poultry industry of the United States will help to bring an appreciation of its importance. Each year there are nearly 300 million chickens raised for egg production in the United States. They produce about 65 billion eggs a year. More than three billion fryers or broilers—the chicken found most commonly in food stores—are grown each year in large commercial flocks. There is no record of the additional millions of eggs and chickens produced in units too small to be counted. There also are millions of roasting chickens, capons, and other chickens grown, to say nothing of approximately 120 million turkeys a year.

While the individual unit—chicken or egg—is small, these figures show that the total volume is tremendous, thus accounting for the importance of the poultry industry.

As the industry has grown in volume, it also has changed in other ways. The gap between small and large flocks has become much wider. Whereas most of the poultry and eggs once were produced in flocks of a few hundred birds on general farms, that is no longer true.

The bulk of the poultry products on the market now comes from large specialized operations which may number hundreds of thousands—even millions—of chickens under one management. This shift has been made possible by the development of highly productive birds of notable uniformity, complete feeds, improved equipment, and more skillful poultry managers.

Marketing regulations, especially the sanitation requirements for dressing large numbers of chickens, also have played a large part in moving poultry production into large units under highly specialized management.

Rather than limiting the opportunities for small producers, however, the trend to large units actually has provided new opportunities, especially in egg production. While the quality of eggs sold in food stores has undergone tremendous improvement, there are large numbers of consumers who still like to buy eggs direct from the farm. But the large commercial operators "can't be bothered" with selling direct to individual buyers. There also are other marketing opportunities which we shall describe in Chapter 9.

As the changes in flock size have occurred, so have there been shifts among the states where chickens and eggs are produced. In 1939 the ten leading states in egg production were Iowa, Texas, California, Pennsylvania, Missouri, Minnesota, Ohio, Illinois, New York, and Wisconsin. Thirty-five years later, the top ten were California, Georgia, Arkansas, Pennsylvania, North Carolina, Alabama, Florida, Indiana, Minnesota, and Texas.

Poultry meat production has undergone an even greater shift in the area of production. In 1939 broiler production was in its infancy and the ten leading states in chickens raised were Iowa, Texas, Illinois, Missouri, Ohio, Minnesota, Pennsylvania, Indiana, California, and Kansas. Again, 35 years later, the ten leaders in broiler production were Arkansas, Georgia, Alabama, North Carolina, Mississippi, Maryland, Texas, Delaware, California, and Maine.

Not all poultry raisers are as successful as those mentioned previously, of course. Chickens probably require a more highly specialized knowledge than any other livestock to get the best from them; conversely, many farmers have found that they pay better for the skill and labor invested.

Perhaps it is this requirement for specialized knowledge which makes it possible for so many people with little agricultural experience to become successful with chickens. Because they recognize their lack of knowledge, they are willing to study the latest books, bulletins and magazines, and to follow directions carefully. It is commonly said that the greatest testing period for a poultryman comes after a year or two of success. It is then that he tends to become careless and to feel that he may violate some of the rules of good management without paying the price. If, as a consequence of his carelessness, he runs into trouble, it is then that he is most likely to become discouraged and lose interest. Those willing to learn and benefit by a setback at that stage, however, usually "make a go" of it.

Some poultry raisers may appear to have continued "bad luck." When observed closely, however, the "bad luck" usually is seen to be the result of poor management or lack of foresight.

First, then, the would-be poultryman must be willing to study about poultry and to learn from the experiences of others. This applies equally to the town backlotter or to the farmer. Actually, the farmer who has been accustomed to keeping a few chickens without giving them much attention may be under a greater handicap because he is able to raise a few fryers and to produce a few eggs throughout the year with a minimum of effort, and fails to realize the benefits to be derived from scientific care.

A second qualification which the would-be poultryman must have is that of stick-to-itiveness, for chickens are likely to require care every day in the year. A garden can be left without care for a few days, but a poultry flock left a half day without water or a full day without feed may require days or weeks to make full recovery.

While a farm has some advantages in the space it provides for rearing young birds and even for the flock of laying hens, yet large space is not a primary factor in successful poultry production. There are successful poultry businesses occupying only a few city lots. In other instances, people are rearing fine broilers or keeping a few laying hens in cages in their basement or in a garage with complete success.

The town poultry raiser, of course, should be sure that zoning regulations or ordinances permit him to keep chickens. Even when he is legally allowed to have them, common courtesy requires that they be housed in such a way that they will not be offensive to neighbors. This usually means keeping no male birds or roosters beyond the fryer stage, because of the disturbance caused by their crowing.

But what can be expected of a small flock in the way of food, whether it is in town or on a farm? This will vary about as much as the gasoline mileage different drivers get from their cars—and for somewhat similar reasons.

Probably the smallest flock to be considered is one numbering 12 to 15 hens, the number suggested for the smallest housing unit shown in Chapter 3. Such a flock, of good laying stock, which could be handled by practically any family under average conditions, would provide about 20 dozen eggs per hen over a period of 12 months after the hens begin laying eggs. The production will not be uniform over the period of lay, however. The hens will lay fewer and smaller eggs as they begin production, will soon reach a peak, then gradually decline throughout the last several months. Superior stock may well do better than this if given good care. Even birds of only fair quality, kept by inexperienced persons, should do two-thirds as well.

Throughout most of the year a flock of this size should produce more eggs than the average family of four or five people can consume, leaving, in many instances, enough for sale to neighbors and friends. Such sales help to pay for the cash expenses of feeding and housing the flock.

If you choose to grow chickens for meat, they should reach an average weight of three pounds or more in seven or eight weeks. So a brood of 50 chicks should produce about 150 pounds of meat. Many owners of small flocks have done this well or better in producing highly nutritious and tasty meat and eggs.

In considering a small flock for meat, however, the decision should not be based wholly on the expectation of saving money. Broiler production is one of those industries in which large-scale operations have a considerable cost advantage. These commercial units have advantages in buying virtually everything they need, but especially in things such as chicks, feed, and equipment. In fact, because the industry is so highly concentrated, it may be difficult to get the right kind of chicks and feed in some areas of the United States due to the limited call for them.

So meat production in small units should be looked at in the same way that you consider a vegetable garden. Even if it doesn't really save any money, it pays rich rewards in the pleasure of working with it and in the freshness and quality of the product.

If you want to produce poultry meat, you might like to consider starting with a brood or two of broilers, then try growing out some roasters and capons. These larger chickens provide superb eating but they may be less generally available than broilers in the food stores and also may be comparatively more expensive.

A small flock of laying hens is more likely to be rewarding financially. But again other values must be considered, as pointed out at the beginning of this chapter. There can be values in by-products too. Poultry manure is an excellent garden fertilizer when properly handled. Meat of a quality different than broilers also is provided by the hens after they have finished their period of egg production. Then as you learn and gain experience, you can look more carefully at the possibility of expanding your flock to a size which can be counted on for worthwhile income.

Yes, there is no doubt about the contribution which a small flock can make toward providing a good living for the average family in town or country and the opportunity for building such a flock into a profitable business. The question is, "How do I go about it?" And that is what we shall attempt to answer in the following chapters.

2

How to Get Started

Once you have decided that you definitely want to have the pleasure and food which a small flock of chickens can provide, the next question is how to get started.

WHERE TO GET SUPPLIES

One of the first things is to find out where the necessary equipment and supplies can be secured. It is just as necessary to know this as to know where to get gasoline and oil for your automobile. In some small towns and suburban communities, there is what is known as a baby chick hatchery. Its principal business is to hatch and sell baby chicks, but most hatcheries also sell feed and practically all kinds of supplies needed by poultry raisers.

But there are other sources of supplies too. Stores specializing in the sale of feed for poultry, livestock, and pets also frequently sell poultry equipment. Many hardware stores carry poultry equipment. Some grocery stores sell poultry feed, and most drugstores maintain at least a small stock of disinfectants and remedies which are needed by poultry raisers.

In some of the larger cities, department stores have set aside a section devoted to the needs of poultrymen. Then, too, there are many companies which sell all kinds of supplies by mail order. Therefore, the fact that there may not be a hatchery or other specialized poultry supply store near you need not hinder you at all in getting just what you need.

There are four main stages in the life of chickens at which you may start. These are hatching eggs, baby chicks, started chicks, or mature pullets (young hens). Since each requires a little different equipment and management, we shall consider them in the order named.

HATCHING EGGS

Not so many years ago the purchase of hatching eggs was quite popular, but today this probably is the least common method of starting a small flock, and properly so. To start with the purchase of hatching eggs requires that they be incubated for three weeks, and you probably will have plenty to learn without adding this very specialized task at the outset. Later on, if you are successful with the other phases of poultry raising, you may want to try this too, but let that come after you have learned how to rear and manage the chickens properly. As a matter of fact, nearly all of the baby chicks raised in the United States are purchased from hatcheries, so there is little reason why a small-flock owner should try to hatch his own.

If, in the beginning, or later, you do wish to purchase hatching eggs, purchase them from a breeder who makes a specialty of selling eggs for hatching. He should have the same qualifications, which will be described later, as for a person selling baby chicks. Don't ever just buy some eggs from a farmer or from your market as you would buy eggs to eat. Many farmers and large poultry raisers do not keep any male birds in their flocks, and therefore, eggs from these flocks would not be fertile and would not hatch. Even if they were fertile, you would have little idea as to the kind of chicks they would be likely to produce.

There are two ways of incubating eggs—with hens or with an incubator. While it might seem reasonable to think that the hen could do the best job of hatching her eggs, you ought to be warned that a setting hen can be one of the most troublesome creatures on earth. Chicken eggs must be incubated for three weeks. Many a hen gets discouraged and walks off the job before that time is up. Some of them are clumsy and break the eggs. In any case, they have to be fed and watered, provided with a comfortable nest, and kept free of lice by dusting them with a louse powder once or twice during the incubation period. One hen can incubate about 13 to 15 eggs.

Incubators holding anywhere from about 50 eggs up to 75,000 can be purchased. Most of them are heated automatically by electricity. If you do not happen to have electric current available, incubators can be purchased which are heated with kerosene lamps.

The incubator ought to be operated in a room which can be kept at a temperature of around 60 to 70 degrees Fahrenheit and well ventilated. The instructions of the manufacturer should be followed very carefully in operating the machine. In general, however, the temperature must be maintained accurately at around 100 degrees Fahrenheit, depending upon the exact type of incubator. It also is important to maintain a fairly high degree of moisture—around 50 to 60 percent relative humidity—in the incubator by the means which will be outlined in the operating instructions. The eggs should be "turned,'"that is, have their position changed, at least two or three times a day, and more often if possible. In small machines, this will have to be done by hand, and it will be all right to leave the eggs out of the incubator in a warm room long enough to turn them. Larger machines have automatic turning devices or hand devices which make it possible to turn all of the eggs quickly at one time.

So you see there is quite a bit to learn in order to do the incubating job properly, and beginners probably are well-advised to leave the incubating job to a hatcheryman who specializes in that phase of the business.

There are a couple of exceptions to the recommendation against attempting to do your own hatching. Incubating eggs can provide an especially interesting demonstration for children. The operation fits into a science class or as a project for a group of youngsters. Some museums maintain a continuous show of chicks emerging from their shells and find that it is one of the best attention-getting displays that they have. It is particularly appropriate during the Easter season.

Small incubators especially adapted for this purpose are available. They have a glass front or top through which the hatching process can be observed without opening the machine. If you have young children in your family or are working with groups of children, the value of such a demonstration may be a consideration in deciding whether to try hatching your own chicks.

If you get into the hobby of showing birds in competition and would like to mate your stock, you also may want to do your own hatching. In fact, it probably would be difficult to find anyone else to do it for you.

But home hatching has too many problems for the small operator to make it desirable simply to produce chicks for a small flock of layers or meat birds.

DAY-OLD CHICKS

There are several ages at which chicks can be bought. Historically, most chicks were bought at day-old. Some were also bought at three to six weeks of age—after they had been well started. Gradually, however, there has been a strong trend to buying ready-to-lay pullets. We shall try to point out the major advantages and disadvantages of each of these three stages.

Day-old chicks are those which have just hatched. They cost less than chicks of the other two ages, of course, but they do require suitable brooding equipment and attentive care. If bought for egg-laying, there will be a period of five or six months before there is any income in the form of eggs for consumption or sale.

But if you will give them proper care, day-old chicks probably require less total investment than chicks of other ages. They also provide the satisfactions inherent in caring for any baby animals.

In some areas chick hatcheries may be rather widely scattered, so you will have to locate them through a local feed dealer, your county agent, or another poultryman. You also can locate hatcheries through the advertisements in poultry publications.

Baby chicks may be shipped a considerable distance because of an unusual feature. About the last thing a chick does before it breaks out of the shell is to draw the yolk of the egg into its body. This material provides sufficient food to nourish the chick for about 72 hours after it hatches. Since the chicks can be packed in specially designed boxes and shipped as soon as they are well dried after hatching, they can travel a long way before needing food and water. However, the sooner they are put into a warm environment with food and water, the better.

If there is a hatchery near you which has the kind of chicks you want, it is wise to go get them at the hatchery. Frequently, hatcheries will deliver sizable orders over a reasonable distance by truck. If you want only a few chicks, you might be able to participate in this service by combining your order with the orders of other poultrymen near you.

When chicks are hatched, of course, they are about half pullets (females) and half cockerels (males). By various means, the hatchery can separate the sexes immediately after hatching. If you are buying chicks for meat, you will want the straight run—both pullets and cockerels. But if you want them for egg production, you will want pullets only. The cockerels of the egg breeds are usually destroyed by the hatchery. So you should expect to pay at least twice as much for pullet chicks only as for straight run.

Because the cockerels can be had for little or nothing, beginners may be tempted to buy straight run chicks of the egg breeds with the idea of growing the cockerels for meat. This would be a mistake except under the most unusual circumstances of very low feed prices or a scarcity of meat. They simply are not bred to put on meat economically and would never make the standard three- or four-pound broiler.

Cockerels and pullets of the meat breeds usually sell at the same price and are bought as straight run.

In selecting a source of chicks, you may find a choice of several hatcheries, each selling a different strain or brand of chicks. The brand name refers to the basic breeder, who corresponds to the basic manufacturer of other products. It may not be easy to make a choice, so follow the same practice you would in making other major purchases. Visit people who have been keeping chickens for some time and ask their advice. As with dealers in other products, sometimes service and willingness to give counsel are as important as the particular brand offered.

In addition to reading advertising and sales material of breeders and hatcherymen and consulting other poultrymen, there is another source of information about the qualities of various strains of stock. This is the report of the Random Sample Tests conducted in several states. In the egg-production tests, a random sample of a breeder's stock is raised and kept through a year of egg production. Traits such as efficiency of feed, number, size, and quality of eggs laid, and other economic factors are recorded and reported. The reports may be carried in poultry publications and an annual summary is published by the Poultry Research Branch, U. S. Department of Agriculture, Beltsville, Maryland 20705.

Most breeders are quite specific about the qualities of their stock, simplifying the problem of making a selection. In selecting a source of stock, also be sure that the breeding flocks are blood tested for pullorum-typhoid. These diseases are transmitted from parents to offspring through the egg. Breeding birds which carry the diseases can be identified by blood testing and removed from the flock. All major breeders carry on a sound program of testing but caution should be used in buying stock of any age when you are not sure of the source. Blood testing should not be forgotten when hatching from your own stock or exchanging with other small operators.

There is a National Poultry Improvement Plan which serves as a supervisory agency (through state agencies) of the breeding and blood-testing programs of many breeders and hatcherymen. Information about the plan may be secured from the Poultry Research Branch mentioned above.

STARTED CHICKS

If you don't have good brooding facilities or can't give day-old chicks the care they need, you may be able to buy chicks a few weeks old. At one time, many hatcheries served their customers by starting chicks for three to six weeks. Along with the other changes in the poultry industry, however, this practice has almost disappeared.

It is mentioned here only because there still may be started chicks available in some locations, and they do have the advantage of requiring less stringent brooding requirements. But they still must have good care, especially since they are being transferred from the environment in which they were started to the one which you will provide. They will need close attention to help them make the adjustment to their new quarters.

As you would expect, started chicks will cost proportionately more than day-old chicks. It should be obvious also that there is no merit in buying started chicks for broiler production.

READY-TO-LAY PULLETS

The fourth way of making a start is by buying pullets when they are just about ready to begin laying eggs. Such pullets are most commonly about 20 weeks old but may range between 16 and 22 weeks. This has become a very popular method of buying egg production stock, especially for a medium-sized flock. It is a suitable method for flocks of any size.

The main advantage here is that all brooding and rearing has been eliminated for you, and you will start getting a return in the form of eggs almost immediately. This adds to your interest in the flock. It also means that your income starts promptly if you are producing eggs to sell.

Of course, the individual birds will cost more at this stage than at any other, but if your interest is in a laying flock only, this method should receive serious consideration. Many breeders and hatcherymen set aside special farms on which to grow pullets, so such birds are generally available in all sections of the country. They may not be available at all times of the year, however, as day-old chicks are. If you want only a few, you may be able to arrange with a nearby poultryman to supply your needs when he buys a large number of pullets for his own flock. If you want several hundred or thousands, it will be best to make arrangements to get them directly from the grower. He will usually deliver such orders within a reasonable distance from his farm.

If you aren't necessarily interested in getting the highest possible egg production, but would like to have both eggs and meat for home use, some pullets of one of the dual-purpose breeds might be a good buy. I remember with pleasure a nice flock of White Plymouth Rock pullets bought in the fall at a slight premium over the market price. They laid at a good rate all winter; we ate a few; and I sold them on the market the following April for an average of about 30 cents a hen more than I had paid for them six months previously! The secret of this gain is found in the fact that the pullets continue to gain in weight throughout the winter and that the market price of hens usually is highest in the spring.

Balancing the quick return from ready-to-lay pullets is their higher cost. If you buy direct from the grower, you probably will be asked to make partial payment with your order and the remainder on delivery.

Sometimes it is possible to buy hens which have laid for a year and are being sold to make room for a new flock. This can be a fine way to get a small flock at relatively low cost, but you must be extremely careful in buying such birds. If you are dealing with a trustworthy farmer or poultryman, he will advise you honestly as to the quality of the birds, how to handle them, and what you may expect from them. If they are still laying eggs, they must be moved carefully, and it is desirable to give them. as nearly as possible, the same feed and care they have been getting. Some or all of them may stop laying for a time and molt (lose their old feathers and grow new ones), then begin laying again. Some will keep on laying without a pause. Such hens (commonly called yearlings and "spent hens") usually will lay approximately two-thirds as many eggs in their second year as they laid during their first year. Some will do much better than that. They also will lay larger eggs as an average than they laid in their first year.

One special caution: do not buy hens from a dealer in market poultry. Do not buy "culls"—hens which are being sold because of poor health or poor laying ability.

If you can establish a good relationship with a nearby poultryman and get his best birds each year as he replaces his flock, you can maintain a satisfactory small flock of your own at low cost.

SELECTING A BREED

One of the questions which puzzles many people is the breed to choose. This is understandable when one realizes that there are more than 40 different breeds of poultry, not counting bantams, described in the standard book of the American Poultry Association which gives the generally accepted description of the various breeds and varieties. Some of the breeds have as many as a dozen different varieties, perhaps differing from each other only in such a small item as the shape of the comb. The most common variety differences within a breed, however, are in the color pattern of the feathers.

In choosing a breed and variety, there are a few helpful suggestions to keep in mind.

Consider first the purpose for which you are rearing chickens. In general, there are three such purposes: the production of eggs, the production of meat, and the development of a hobby from which to derive pleasure, as one might breed pedigreed dogs, horses or other animals.

The Leghorn-type strains far outrank all other breeds in popularity for the production of eggs. They are used on the large, commercial egg farms. These strains are derived basically from the Single Comb (abbreviated as S. C.) White Leghorn, which always has been noted for high egg production. Breeders have improved on the basic Leghorn, especially in uniformity, by various methods of inbreeding and crossing, resulting in the "Leghorn-type" designation. These birds may tend to be somewhat more nervous in temperament than the larger breeds, a possible disadvantage in small flocks.

Because they are smaller than most other popular breeds, Leghorns eat less feed and more of them can be housed in a given space. Breeders have further reduced the size of some of the Leghorn-type strains and have increased their efficiency in converting feed into eggs. An-

BREEDS OF POULTRY MOST COMMON IN AMERICA

Breed	Standard Adult Weight		Skin Color	Egg Shell Color
	Male	Female		
Leghorns	6	4½	Yellow	White
(Principal varieties: White, Brown, Buff, Black)				
S. C. Rhode Island Reds	8½	6½	Yellow	Brown
New Hampshires	8½	6½	Yellow	Brown
Plymouth Rocks	9½	7½	Yellow	Brown
(Principal varieties: White, Barred, Buff, Columbian)				
Wyandottes	8½	6½	Yellow	Brown
(Principal varieties: White, Buff, Silver Laced, Columbian)				
Jersey Black Giants	13	10	Yellow	Brown
S. C. Minorcas (White, Buff)	8	6½	White	White
Minorcas (Black)	9	7½	White	White

other factor contributing to their popularity is the preference for white-shelled eggs in most of the United States. Some people prefer brown-shelled eggs, although there is no difference in nutritional value. S.C. Rhode Island Reds, New Hampshires, and Plymouth Rocks are good producers of brown eggs. They also are somewhat larger than Leghorns, more docile, and provide more meat when dressed out. Crosses of these breeds have also been made for egg and meat production.

For broiler production, specially bred strains involving crosses of the heavier breeds are preferred. If one wishes to produce really heavy meat birds, then breeds such as Jersey Black Giants—the heaviest of the standard breeds—or Jersey White Giants should be chosen. The standard weight of the Jersey Black Giant hen is 10 pounds. Capons (males which have been unsexed by removing the sex organs) of this breed may be grown to a weight of 12 to 15 pounds.

But if one is raising chickens for the pleasure to be derived from breeding beautiful birds, and perhaps exhibiting them in competition with other hobbyists (called "fanciers" in the poultry world), the choice of breeds and varieties is practically unlimited. There are literally dozens, varying in size, shape, and plumage color. A visit to the poultry show held in connection with most county and state fairs, or held as separate exhibitions once or twice a year in many cities, will reveal breeds certain to delight your eye. And, even though they may not be common on large commercial egg farms, do not be misled into thinking they will not lay a fair number of eggs. A dozen hens of almost any of the standard breeds will provide an ample supply of eggs for the average family throughout most of the year.

But if you still are undecided, then visit your hatcheryman or other local poultry raisers and inquire which breeds are most popular in your section of the country. You will make no mistake in beginning with a breed which other poultry raisers have found well adapted to your locality. One advantage of chickens is that, if the notion strikes you, it is relatively easy to change breeds, and there certainly is no point in continuing with a breed which you do not like. A liking for one's chickens is one of the most important qualifications for success.

BANTAMS

Instead of keeping any of the breeds of "large" poultry, you may prefer to keep bantams, especially if your flock is to be primarily a hobby or a project for boys or girls.

Bantams are mainly miniatures of the larger breeds, although there are also several distinct breeds of bantams. Most are less than one-

BARRED PLYMOUTH ROCKS

S. C. WHITE LEGHORNS

S. C. RHODE ISLAND REDS

IDEAL MALE AND FEMALE NEW HAMPSHIRE

As Interpreted by the
New Hampshire Club of America

half as large as the bigger breeds, and, therefore, can be kept in small coops. They eat only about one-fourth to one-third as much feed, but, on the other hand, they do not provide nearly as much meat and lay fewer and smaller eggs than the larger breeds. Most bantam owners figure on using three bantam eggs for two standard-sized eggs in cooking, and so forth.

Bantams are reared and managed in practically the same manner as larger breeds, except that smaller equipment and less feed are required.

TIME OF YEAR TO START

The time of year to make a start with poultry will depend somewhat upon the methods of beginning. If you buy day-old baby chicks or started chicks, then it is best to start in the spring, for they are more readily available then, and rearing conditions are more favorable during the spring and summer. If, however, you want to start with chicks at some other season of the year, there are quite a large number of hatcheries which operate on a year-round basis, particularly for the production of broiler chicks.

If you are beginning with ready-to-lay pullets, they may be purchased at any time of year, but will be most readily available in late summer and fall.

The person equipped to brood chicks properly will do best to buy heavier-breed chicks in March or early April so that they will have ample time to mature by early fall. The light-breed chicks, such as Leghorns, can be purchased in April, or even in May, and still mature in time to be laying in the fall. As you may have observed, eggs are scarcest and highest-priced in the fall of year. For that reason, it is well to start the chicks early enough, so that they will be producing eggs for your use during this fall season. Since it requires about six months for hens to mature—a little longer for the heavier breeds and a little less for the light breeds—this means starting them in the late winter or early spring.

Many farm and commercial poultry raisers start two or three broods of chicks during the year, perhaps starting one in late January or February, a second in April, and a third in October or November. When they have facilities to do this, it provides a constant supply of new pullets for egg production; one or two broods may be used for the rearing of pullets and the remainder for meat production only. This has the further advantage of keeping the brooding equipment in more constant use, instead of for only a relatively small part of the year.

HOW MANY TO ORDER

If you are buying ready-to-lay pullets, you will buy only the exact number which your laying house can take care of comfortably.

If you are buying hatching eggs, it is desirable to buy about five eggs for each good pullet wanted the following fall. On the average, only about two-thirds of the eggs will hatch good chicks, half of the chicks will be cockerels, and some of the chicks will die or will need to be culled out before they reach laying age.

If you buy day-old baby chicks, it is best to figure on about 110 chicks (pullets) for each 100 good hens wanted.

In buying started chicks, the older the chicks the more nearly you can buy the exact number wanted to produce the pullets you can house next fall.

These rules apply for determining the number of chicks to buy for established flocks also. Some poultry raisers buy all new stock each year and sell all of the yearling hens. This probably is the best practice for small-flock owners. Others may keep one-fourth to one-third of the best hens, and, therefore, need pullets to replace only about two-thirds of the hens each fall.

WHEN TO ORDER

Remember that it takes three weeks for eggs to hatch, and a hatchery-man cannot keep a stock of chicks indefinitely as a dry-goods merchant may keep his merchandise. Most hatcherymen determine the number of eggs to set by the number of orders on hand. Therefore, if you want to be sure of getting the breed, quality, and number of chicks at the time you want them, it is advisable to place your order with the hatcheryman at least three weeks before the date you want them. During the peak of the season, from mid-March to mid-May, many hatcherymen are booked to capacity for several weeks in advance; therefore, place your order just as far in advance as you know definitely what you would like to have.

If you plan to get a sizable number of ready-to-lay pullets direct from the grower, order them six months in advance.

Specialized hatcheries use incubators holding up to 75,000 eggs at one time. Operation of these huge incubators is almost completely automatic.

Fine shed-roof house for a good farm flock.

Feeders and fountains for chicks of various ages. Small pans at lower left screw on Mason jars. (National Ideal Co.)

Battery brooders for starting chicks up to age of four to six weeks. Each tier has thermostatically controlled electric hover. (*Hawkins Million Dollar Hen*)

Popular type battery. Chicks are started in top tray and moved to lower trays for growing and finishing. (*Brower Mfg. Co.*)

Low floor type of feeder. Crushed oyster shell or ground limestone is in small compartment at end of feeder. (*Ohio State University*)

When ground area is limited or contaminated by previous broods, a sun porch will provide space and beneficial sunshine.

Satisfactory roosting pit arrangement. Roosts are hinged to back wall so they can be raised and hooked to ceiling. Front panel lifts off so droppings and litter can be shoveled out.

Cardboard brooder arrangement for starting 50 chicks in basement. (It should be at least 28 x 28 inches.) Curtain retains heat in brooder, yet chicks can pass back and forth freely.

Outdoor coop used for finishing 50 chicks started in cardboard brooder. Roosts are in shelter; feeders and water fountain are on wire sun porch.

Lean-to shed on south side of barn provides good shelter for small farm flock. (*G. T. Klein, Mass. State College*)

6 x 8 ft. house with sun porch the same size. Floor of porch is made of 1 by 1 in. strips, one inch apart; sides are of laths; top of poultry netting.

3
Equipment Needed

Equipment for rearing chicks or maintaining a small laying flock can be very simple or it can be as elaborate as you wish. With a little ingenuity and close attention to the fundamentals of good management, many people are successful in rearing chickens or in getting good egg production with little more equipment than that usually found in the average home. Good equipment, however, usually makes success more certain, decreases the labor, and increases the pleasure derived from the flock.

If one expects to have a flock larger than the very minimum necessary to meet the family needs, then some outlay for housing and equipment is practically essential.

Equipment needs may be divided between those of the laying flock and those for brooding and rearing chicks. Although there is some overlapping in the use of such equipment, it probably will be better to consider them separately. It may appear like reversing the natural order, but the needs of a laying flock will be considered first.

A second division in equipment needs is that between the floor system, where the chickens are kept on the floor of the house or allowed to run out in small yards or pens, and the battery system, where the chickens are kept confined in wooden or wire cages, usually several tiers high. The floor system will be considered first.

HOUSE PLANS

The largest item of equipment for a laying flock, of course, is the house. There is little uniformity in the housing provided for small flocks, for the exact shape and size of the house is not particularly important. Consider first what already may be available to you. A garage, or a portion of one, a tool shed, a lean-to, or similar outbuilding can be converted into a satisfactory shelter for hens. The first consideration is that the shelter have a water-tight roof and sides, with windows for light and ventilation. Ventilation also may be provided through adjustable slots at the top of the front wall or by means of roof ventilators with adjustable openings.

It is very desirable to have a rat-proof floor of concrete. For temporary use or where it is essential to save on cash outlay, three or four inches of dirt may be excavated from the floor and the excavation filled with gravel for use as a floor. Even more satisfactory than gravel is a six-inch layer of ground limestone spread over firmly packed soil or used to fill an excavation of the same depth. If dampened and tamped down, it forms a relatively firm surface. Then, since either gravel or ground limestone should be removed and replaced with new material each year, the limestone has the added advantage of being of considerable value when spread on garden or crop land.

Frequently an otherwise desirable building will have a wood floor of single thickness. Such a floor has numerous disadvantages because it usually will be cold, and the space beneath it provides an excellent haven for rats if it is close to the ground, for they can gnaw through it very easily. Furthermore, such a floor tends to warp badly from the moisture present in most poultry houses, and it is difficult to clean thoroughly. Such a floor can be vastly improved by covering it with a layer of building paper, or, better still, with a sheet of insulation board, then laying a second floor at right angles to the first. Six-inch tongue-and-groove flooring can be used for this second floor. It will be better, too, if such a house is raised up on posts, concrete blocks, or bricks so that rats will not harbor under it.

A fundamental in determining housing needs is the floor space necessary for each hen. The general rule is 3 square feet for each hen of the smaller breeds, such as White Leghorns, and 4 square feet for each hen of the larger breeds. Experienced poultrymen have learned, however, that it never pays to crowd chickens, and 3½ square feet even for the smaller breeds will be desirable. About 1 to 1½ square feet per bird probably will suffice for bantams. These space requirements apply regardless of the type of house, as long as the floor system of management is followed.

If a new building must be constructed, then there are numerous good plans available. Again the exact style is not important, although it should be pleasing in appearance. The main thing is to provide a satisfactory shelter at reasonable cost. Although some of the important considerations in locating a new house are discussed in a later chapter, it is well to keep in mind that it ought to be located so that the hens will be kept away from the barnyard (if on a farm) and in a well-drained location.

6-BY-8-FOOT HOUSE

Shown in the following plans is a 6-by-8-foot house, suitable for 12 to 15 hens. It is practical, relatively easy to build, and pleasing in appearance. It is not necessary that a house for a flock this small be any higher, for the caretaker should not have to spend much time inside it. This house is adaptable for the use of a wide variety of materials, ranging from scrap lumber covered with roofing paper, to drop siding or such special materials as insulation hardboard or asbestos siding.

In building this house, it probably would be most convenient to start by building the floor, then building each side and each half of the roof as separate units. All of these finally could be brought together to make the completed structure. The house could be bolted together for easier dismantling if it should be necessary to move it from one location to another. While this house could be built with any of the styles of floors mentioned earlier, we believe that the one shown in the plan probably is most satisfactory for it. If this double wooden floor is used, the house should be set up on bricks, concrete, or wooden blocks to keep it at least six inches above the ground.

One suggestion for possible improvement in this plan is provision for a hinged door along the bottom of the back wall through which the floor litter and droppings could be raked out.

10-BY-12-FOOT SHED-ROOF HOUSE

For a flock of 30 to 40 hens, the 10-by-12-foot shed-roof house is very popular. Because it is necessary to work inside a house of this size, it is built high enough for convenience of the caretaker.

While the cost of the house would be considerably reduced by omitting the insulation board, this insulation will help to make the house much warmer in winter and cooler in summer. It also will make the

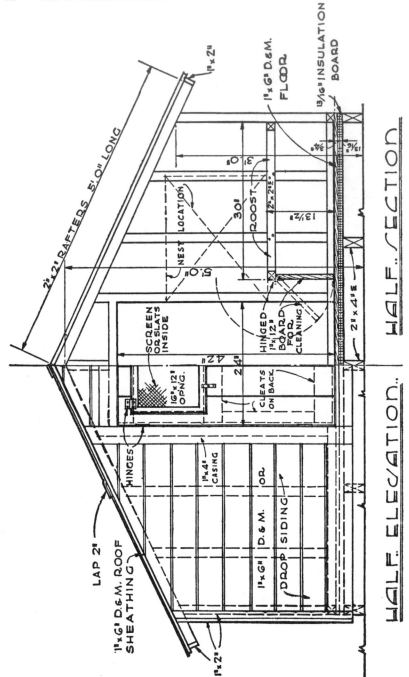

1"x 2"

2"x 2" RAFTERS 5'.0" LONG

1"x G" D.&M.
FLOOR

13/16" INSULATION
BOARD

3'.0"

30'

NEST LOCATION

2"x 2"

ROOST

13 1/2"

3/4"
13 1/2"

SCREEN
OR SLATS
INSIDE

5'.0"

HINGED
1"x 12"
BOARD
FOR
CLEANING

HALF SECTION

2"x 4"s

16"x 12"
OPNG.

42"

24"

CLEATS
ON BACK

LAP 2"

HINGES

1"x 4"
CASING

1"x G" D.&M.
DROP SIDING

OR

1"x G' D.&M. ROOF
SHEATHING

1"x 2"

HALF ELEVATION

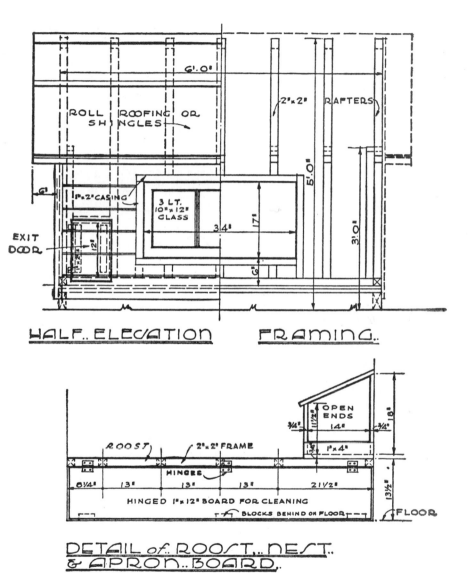

HALF ELEVATION   FRAMING

DETAIL of ROOST, NEST & APRON BOARD

PLANS FOR A 6-BY-8-FOOT HOUSE
(Bill of materials on following page)

BILL OF MATERIALS FOR 6-BY-8-FOOT HOUSE

Floor
> 2 pcs. 2" × 4" × 8' floor sills
> 5 pcs. 2" × 4" × 6' floor joists
> 48 board feet 6" flooring
> 3 pcs. 2' × 8' − 15/16 in. thick t. & g. insulation board sheathing

Front and Back Walls
> 7 pcs. 2" × 2" × 12' plates and studding
> 1 pc. 1" × 6" × 2' window rest
> 1 pc. 1" × 2" × 12' window trim
> 1 pc. 1" × 1" × 12' window stop
> 2 pcs. 4' × 6' structural board for siding or 32 bd. ft. of other siding material

Ends
> 10 pcs. 2" × 2" × 12' plates and studding
> 2 pcs. 4' × 8' structural board for siding or 64 bd. ft. of other siding material

Roof
> 9 pcs. 2" × 2" × 10' rafters
> 2 pcs. 4' × 10' structural board for roof (any one of insulation hardboards well-painted or asbestos boards) or equal amount of other roofing material
> 2 pcs. 1" × 2" × 8'

Finish
> 2 pcs. 1" × 6" × 6' cone boards
> 2 pcs. 1" × 4" × 12' corner boards
> 2 pcs. 1" × 3" × 12' corner boards

Dropping Pit
> 2 pcs. 2" × 2" × 12'
> 1 pc. 1" × 12" × 6'

Nests
> 1 pc. 1" × 8" × 4' for bottom
> 2 pcs. 1" × 6" × 8' sides and top
> 1 pc. 1" × 4" × 3' ends

Hardware and Paint
> 2 pairs 3" butt hinges for ventilator doors
> 1 door latch
> 1 pair 4" strap hinges for door
> 1 pc. 1" poultry netting 2' × 7' for window and ventilators
> 1 pc. poultry netting, $1\frac{1}{2}$" mesh, 16 guage (or as heavy as available) $2\frac{1}{2}$' × 6' under roosts
> 1 lb. 16d nails
> 1 lb. 8d casing nails
> 3 lbs. 1" galv. roofing nails
> $1\frac{1}{2}$ gal. white lead and oil paint

house more satisfactory if used for brooding chicks. The insulation board should be applied on the outside of the studding and on top of the rafters before the siding and sheathing are applied. One objection to insulation board is that chickens sometimes pick

BILL OF MATERIALS FOR 10-BY-12-FOOT SHED-ROOF HOUSE

Dimension Lumber
- 2 pieces, 4″ × 6″, 14 ft. long, for runner
- 7 pieces, 2″ × 4″, 10 ft. long, for joists
- 4 pieces, 2″ × 4″, 12 ft. long, for joists
- 7 pieces, 2″ × 4″, 7 ft. long, for front stud
- 6 pieces, 2″ × 4″, 5 ft. long, for rear stud
- 5 pieces, 2″ × 4″, 14 ft. long, for side stud
- 2 pieces, 2″ × 4″, 10 ft. long, for plate
- 6 pieces, 2″ × 6″, 14 ft. long, for rafter
- 145 feet B.M. 1″ × 8″, shiplap, first layer of floor
- 145 feet B.M. 1″ × 6″, flooring, 12 ft. length
- 200 feet B.M. 1″ × 8″, shiplap roof sheathing
- 340 feet B.M. 1″ × 6″ drop siding
- 420 sq. ft. insulation
- 2 pieces 1″ × 2″, 10 ft. long, muslin window frames
- 3 pieces 1″ × 4″, 10 ft. long, window sill and casing
- 2 pieces ³/₄″ × ³/₄″, 12 ft. long, quarter round
- 1 piece 1″ × 4″, 16 ft., for corner boards
- 1 piece 1″ × 3″, 16 ft., for corner boards
- 1 piece 1″ × 3″, 12 ft., for corner boards
- 1 piece 1″ × 4″, 12 ft., for corner boards
- 1 piece 1″ × 6″, 14 ft., for door frame
- 2 pieces 1″ × 4″, 16 ft., for verge board

Hardware, Roofing, Sash, etc.
- 1¹/₂ squares building paper for floor
- 2 rolls prepared roofing
- 4 4-light 10″ × 12″ sash
- 18 linear ft., 1″ mesh poultry netting, 30″ wide
- 8 extra heavy strap hinges, 4″
- 2 extra heavy strap hinges, 6″
- 1 door latch
- 4 butt hinges, 3″
- 2 yds. muslin (or glass substitute)
- 10 lbs. 6d nails
- 5 lbs. 8d nails
- 5 lbs. 10d nails
- 2 lbs. 20d nails
- ¹/₄ lb. poultry netting staples
- 16 window spring bolts

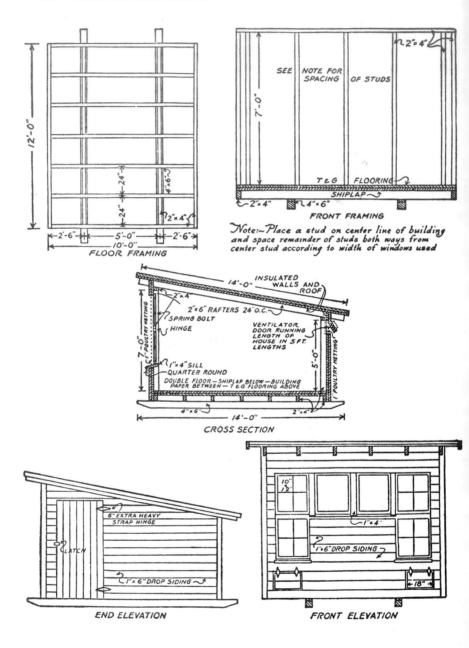

FLOOR FRAMING

FRONT FRAMING

Note:—Place a stud on center line of building and space remainder of studs both ways from center stud according to width of windows used

CROSS SECTION

END ELEVATION

FRONT ELEVATION

PLANS FOR A 10-BY-12-FOOT SHED-ROOF HOUSE
(Bill of materials on preceding page)

through it, especially the softer, untreated kinds. This can be avoided by covering it with cheap lumber or hardboard a few feet high or wherever the chickens can reach it. Another method of protection is to paint it with two or three coats of hard, glossy paint, first using a primer-sealer. Some tests indicate that gray color is most effective in preventing picking.

Many people like this house in a 12-by-12-foot or 12-by-14-foot size, and these larger sizes can be built from the same plan by simply extending the walls. These larger sizes unquestionably have some advantages for farm use and are to be preferred there.

Ventilation in these smaller houses can be secured through the windows or special ventilator openings shown in the plans. The windows should be of a type which either slides up and down in channels or which tilts inward at the top. Another style of window well liked is one hinged at the top and swinging to the outside. This gives greater protection from rain, but it must be fastened firmly when opened to avoid having it blown off by the wind. The window openings should be covered with wire netting of one-inch mesh.

20-BY-40-FOOT SHED-ROOF HOUSE

For the farm flock or for a flock expected to furnish considerable cash income on a small acreage, a house 20 by 40 feet in size is most popular. This will house 250 hens comfortably. Some poultry raisers put 300 hens in a house this size, but that really is overcrowding them.

A shed-roof house should not be built wider than 20 feet, especially in the northern states where heavy snows occur. A house much narrower in width is not considered as satisfactory to ventilate and does not give as good protection for the birds. Also the narrower the house, the more expensive it is to build according to floor space.

Since a concrete floor is almost always used in a house of this size, it is helpful to slope it about four inches from rear to front. This slope is not noticeable in working in the house, yet if rain should happen to blow in through the windows, it will drain back toward the front of the house. Also if floor drains are placed in the front of the house, it then becomes a simple matter to scrub the entire floor and have the water drain to a convenient point. Another advantage of a sloping floor is that the litter will tend to remain in front of the house instead of being scratched back under the dropping boards as it usually is.

For larger flocks a variety of house styles are used. A popular floor system in the Midwest uses a house 30 feet wide and 100 feet long for each 1,000 hens. It is commonly 220 feet long, the center 20 feet being used for a feed room.

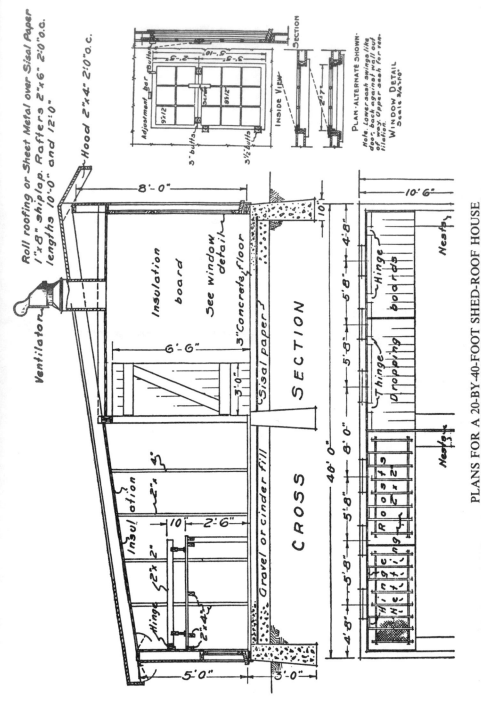

Roll roofing or Sheet Metal over Sisal Paper
1"x8" shiplap. Rafters 2"x6" 2'0"o.c.
lengths 10'-0" and 12'0"

Hood 2"x4" 2'0" o.c.

Ventilator

8'-0"

Insulation board

See window detail

3" Concrete floor

Sisal paper

6'-6"

3'-0"

2"x 4"

Insulation

10" 2'-6"

Hinge 2"x 2"

2"x4"

Gravel or cinder fill

5'-0"   3'-0"

CROSS   SECTION

Adjustment bar

9½"   Screen   9½"

5"-2"   5'-10"

3'-3½"

3" butts   3½" butts

INSIDE VIEW

SECTION

2"x4"

PLAN - ALTERNATE SHOWN

Note. Lower sash swings like door, back against wall out of way. Upper sash for ventilation.

WINDOW DETAIL
Scale 3/4"=1'-0"

10'-6"

10"

4'-8"   5'-8"   5'-8"   8'-0"   5'-8"   5'-8"   4'-8"

40'-0"

Hinge

Dropping boards

Hinge

Nests

Nests

Roosts 2"x 2"

Hinge Netting

PLANS FOR A 20-BY-40-FOOT SHED-ROOF HOUSE

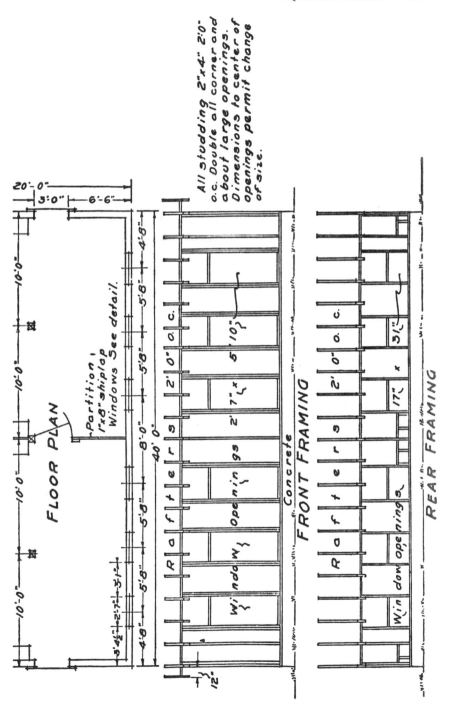

All studding 2"x4" 2'0"
o.c. Double all corner and
about large openings.
Dimensions to center of
openings permit change
of size.

FLOOR PLAN

Partition
1"x8" shiplap
Windows See detail.

FRONT FRAMING

Rafters   2'0" o.c.

Window Openings   2'7" x   5'10"

Concrete

REAR FRAMING

Rafters   2'0" o.c.

Window openings   17" x   31"

BILL OF MATERIALS FOR 20-BY-40-FOOT SHED-ROOF LAYING HOUSE

Concrete

Foundation wall 10 cu. yds. 1:2:4 mix requires 64 bags cement, 9 cu. yds. gravel and $4\frac{1}{2}$ cu. yds. sand.

Floor

$6\frac{2}{3}$ cu. yds. 1:2:4 mix requires 40 bags cement, 6 cu. yds. gravel and 3 cu. yds. sand. Gravel or cinder fill, 13 cu. yds.

Sills

6 pieces 2″ × 4″ × 20′-0″

Studding

20 pieces 2″ × 4″ × 16′-0″ cut
10 pieces 2″ × 4″ × 10′-0″ cut (rear)
12 pieces 2″ × 4″ × 14′-0″ ends

Girder

3 pieces 4″ × 4″ × 6′-0″

Posts

4 pieces 2″ × 6″ × 20′-0″

Plate

4 pieces 2″ × 4″ × 20′-0″

Rafters

21 pieces 2″ × 6″ × 12′-0″ rear
21 pieces 2″ × 6″ × 10′-0″ front
23 pieces 2″ × 4″ × 2′-0″ hood
2 pieces 2″ × 4″ × 22′-0″ verge

Roof sheathing

1200 bd. ft. shiplap 1″ × 8″ (includes extra for dropping board)

Roofing

10 squares
Alternate for sheet metal roof: 26 Ga. $1\frac{1}{4}$″ corrugated, Seal of Quality
Front, 22 pieces 2′ lengths. (Cut 6 pieces 8′0)
Rear, 8′ plus 8′ plus 7′ lengths
    44 pieces 8′, 22 pieces 7′ lengths
5 10′ lengths of ridge roll, 14″ girth, copper bearing, 28 gauge.
If metal is used, 400 bd. ft. 1″ × 4″ fence siding for lath to fasten sheet metal to can be substituted for 1,000 bd. ft. shiplap sheathing.

Siding

1000 bd. ft. No. 116 1″ × 6″ (includes material for doors)
Alternate for sheet metal siding:
Front 10 pieces 9′ lengths, 9 pcs. 3′ lengths.
    (Cut 3 pcs. 9′)
Rear 13 pieces 6′ lengths, 9 pcs. 4′ lengths.
    (Cut 5 pcs. 8′)
Ends 5 pieces 8′ lengths, 5 pcs. 6′ lengths.
    Double this item.

Total sheet metal required for roofing and siding, $16\frac{1}{2}$ squares.
Use 28 guage, Seal of Quality, 2 oz. coating for siding.

Insulation
1500 sq. ft.

Sisal Paper
1800 sq. ft.

Casing
240 ln. ft. $1'' \times 4''$
48 ln. ft. $1'' \times 6''$
96 ln. ft. $1'' \times 3''$

Sash
6 9-light $9'' \times 12'' \times 1\frac{3}{8}''$
6 6-light $9'' \times 12'' \times 1\frac{3}{8}''$
6 3-light $9'' \times 12'' \times 1\frac{3}{8}''$

Hardware
80 ln. ft. $30''$ netting, $1\frac{1}{2}$ mesh, 16 gauge
$16-\frac{1}{2}'' \times 8\frac{1}{2}''$ wagon bolts (to support roost stringers)
$16-\frac{3}{8}'' \times 10''$ bolts–sills
20 lbs. 16d nails
30 lbs. 8d nails
15 lbs. 6d nails
5 lbs. 6d finishing nails
25 lbs. $1\frac{1}{2}''$ galv. roofing nails (insulation)
Add if metal roofing and siding used:
30 lbs. $2''$ screw drive lead head galvanized nails for metal roofing
and siding
3 pairs $5''$ hinges
6 pairs $3\frac{1}{2}''$ butts galv.
6 pairs $3''$ butts galv.
6 pairs $2\frac{1}{2}''$ butts galv.
8 pairs 5T-hinges
3 hasps and staples
3 door hooks

Paint
3 gallons lead and oil
1 gallon boiled linseed oil
1 quart turpentine

Most large flocks are on wire cages, however, rather than on the floor. There are several types and arrangements of cages; so when you are ready to expand, consult your state-college poultry specialists or other authorities as to those preferred currently. They include automatic watering and sometimes automatic feeding and egg gathering.

You may be able to buy a section of used cages from a poultryman disposing of his equipment if you want to try them.

Poultrymen usually like to incorporate their own ideas in houses of large size, although basic plans for such houses may be secured from state agricultural colleges, poultry magazines, feed companies, and other agencies.

Poultry houses of all types and sizes should be well insulated, especially in the northern states. Insulation keeps the house warmer, thus making ventilation easier, and these two, in turn, help to keep the litter drier. The common insulating boards are easiest to use, particularly in a new building where they can be nailed on the outside of the studding. As previously mentioned the soft type should be protected from pecking by the chickens. Foam insulation in plastic board form is waterproof (but not peckproof or ratproof), light in color, and easy to apply.

Good insulation, with a vapor barrier and natural or forced (fan) ventilation, is a necessity if a house is to be kept reasonably dry during cold weather.

YARD OR SUN PORCH

For small flocks of chicks and laying hens, a small outside pen will be desirable. This can be simply a fenced-in enclosure in front of the house, using poultry netting 5 or 6 feet high. If the top of the pen can be covered over with netting, the sides may be 2 or 3 feet high.

While this may seem to be the simplest arrangement, it is not generally the most satisfactory. The chickens usually will pick the ground bare of grass, after which it will be dusty or muddy and generally unsightly. After chickens have been kept on it for a year or two, it will have the further disadvantage of being a source of infection for various poultry diseases and parasites.

Better than a yard such as this is a completely enclosed pen, commonly known as a sun porch. This can have a floor of welded wire or 1-by-1-inch wooden strips set up 10 to 12 inches above the ground so that the manure can be cleaned out from under it. Such a porch does not need to be more than 2 feet high, and the sides can be made of wire or lath. The top, likewise, can be of wire or lath. With a 6-by-8-

foot house, the porch area can be the same size. This will enable the chickens to get out into the sunlight and will provide practically all of the benefits of a yard without the disadvantages.

It should be clearly understood that this recommendation is primarily for very small flocks, especially on a limited acreage. Most specialized poultrymen keep their hens confined to the laying house at all times.

LAYING-HOUSE EQUIPMENT

Inside each house there must be certain basic equipment.

Roosts—These can be the conventional roosts and dropping boards as shown in the plan for the 20-by-40-foot house, or what is known as dropping pits, as shown in the 6-by-8-foot house plan. Dropping pits are much to be preferred in the small houses and many poultrymen believe they are more convenient and save labor even in the larger houses. Dropping boards ought to be cleaned at least twice a week, while dropping pits can be cleaned every few months or as often as the floor litter is removed. Contrary to expectations, dropping pits are not offensive, but if they should become so in very humid weather, sprinkling a little superphosphate or hydrated lime over the droppings will help eliminate any offensive odor and will add to the fertilizing value of the droppings. If superphosphate or hydrated lime are not available, wood ashes or even sand or fine soil may be used.

The necessary roosting space is about 7 inches per bird for Leghorns, 10 inches per bird for the medium-sized breeds such as Plymouth Rocks, and 12 to 14 inches for the very large breeds, such as Brahmas or Jersey Black Giants. Place the roosts 14 to 16 inches apart, depending on the size of the birds. The hens should be kept out of the droppings by the use of 1-by-4-inch welded wire cloth or 1½ -inch mesh, 16 guage, poultry netting nailed to the underside of the roosts and extending down in front to keep the hens from going under the roosts. If wire is not available, lath or 1-by-1-inch wooden strips may be used. Roosts most commonly used are 2-by-2-inch material, with the upper corners slightly rounded.

Nests—Nests must be provided in which the hens may lay their eggs. Since, in the average flock, most hens lay in the morning, there should be plenty of nests. One nest for every five hens is about right. For light breeds, a nest 11 by 12 inches is a good size, but birds of the heavier breeds should have nests 1 or 2 inches larger than this. Many poultrymen, large and small, use orange crates as nests, as shown in the accompanying plan. Metal nests also are popular and have an advantage in being easier to keep free of mites.

A type of nest very desirable, especially in the small houses, is what is known as the "tunnel" nest, which has no partitions. The hens may enter and leave at either end, and a hinged board along the front makes it convenient to gather the eggs. In the plan of the 6-by-8-foot house the eggs are gathered from one end of the nest and no hinged board is necessary. Hens usually do less crowding on nests of this type.

Feeders—There are many good types of feeders, but for the very small flock a feeder from which the chickens may eat while standing

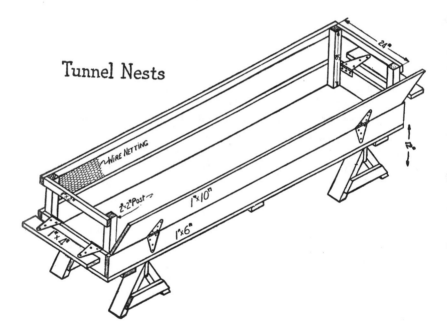

Tunnel Nests

A box "tunnel" nest 8 feet long which will accommodate a flock of 100 hens. It should be covered over the top and mounted near the wall with enough air space in back to provide ventilation. The eggs can be reached by opening the hinged board in front. The hens enter at either end. (*Ohio Agricultural Experiment Station*) on the floor or on a low step is probably most satisfactory. Feeders on legs and hanging tubular feeders also are popular for flocks of all sizes. They are easy to fill and open up the floor space.

There should be at least one linear foot of feeding space for each ten hens, provided they can eat from both sides of the feeder. Many poultrymen provide one foot for each six to eight hens. Never be afraid of providing too much feeding space, for heavy feed consumption is necessary for high egg production.

Water Fountains—A fountain of at least one-gallon capacity is needed for 12 to 15 hens if it is to be filled only once a day. In larger flocks, it can be figured that each 100 hens in heavy production will require about seven gallons of water daily. Of course, running water with float valves to maintain a constant supply usually is provided in larger houses.

EQUIPMENT FOR REARING CHICKS

House—As with hens, the major piece of equipment for rearing chicks is a house. This can be the same house as is used for the hens. In fact, the person beginning with chickens can determine the type of house he wants for his hens, then use that same house in which to brood the chicks and rear the first flock of pullets.

The size of the brooder house will determine the number of chicks which can be raised in one brood. The general recommendation is to allow about one-third to one-half square foot of floor space per chick up to the age of six weeks, at which time the floor space needs to be doubled, perhaps moving half the pullets to a range shelter. This means that the 6-by-8-foot house would be suitable for starting about 100 chicks and a 10-by-12-foot house suitable for about 250. Not more than 300 to 350 chicks should be started in one unit, regardless of the size of the house. This may seem like entirely too much space when the chicks are first put into the house, but remember that the 100 chicks which weigh approximately eight pounds when you get them will weigh around 250 pounds 10 weeks later.

The pullets will need about one square foot of floor space per bird to grow them to maturity, even when a sun porch or outside range is provided. If they must be confined to the brooder house only, they will need double this amount of space by the time they are three or four months old.

In the second year, it will be necessary to provide a separate room for rearing the chicks, but by starting the chicks in the laying house the first year, the initial investment can be held down materially. The brooder house in later years can be the 6-by-8-foot or 10-by-12-foot

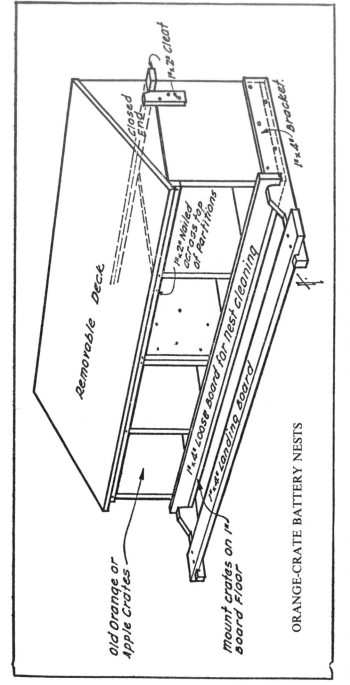

Closed End

1"x2" Cleat

1"x4" Bracket.

Removable Deck

1"x2" Nailed across top of partitions

1"x4" Loose Board for nest cleaning

1"x4" Landing board

Old Orange or Apple Crates

Mount crates on 1" Board Floor

ORANGE-CRATE BATTERY NESTS

Plans for a nest using old orange or apple crates. If these are not available, a similar style of nest can be made using 1-inch lumber. The nests may be three tiers high, if desired. An improvement would be to have the landing board hinged so it could be turned up in front of the nests at night, preventing any hens from roosting in them.

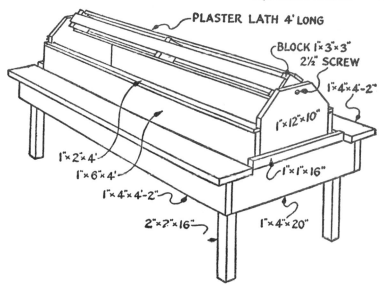

PLASTER LATH 4' LONG

BLOCK 1"x3"x3"
2½" SCREW
1"x4"x4'-2"
1"x12"x10"
1"x1"x16"
1"x2"x4'
1"x6"x4'
1"x4"x4'-2"
2"x2"x16"
1"x4"x20"

Complete dimensions for homemade mash feeder. It is 4 feet long and will accommodate about 40 hens.

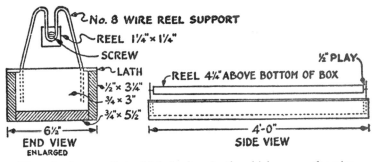

No. 8 WIRE REEL SUPPORT
REEL 1¼"x 1¼"
SCREW
LATH
½ PLAY
REEL 4¼" ABOVE BOTTOM OF BOX
½"x 3¼"
¾ x 3"
¾"x 5½"
6½
END VIEW
ENLARGED
4'-0"
SIDE VIEW

Plans for intermediate-chick feeder. As the chicks grow, the wire reel supports can be raised.

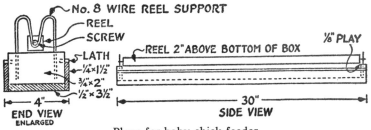

No. 8 WIRE REEL SUPPORT
REEL
SCREW
½" PLAY
LATH
REEL 2" ABOVE BOTTOM OF BOX
¼"x1½
¾"x2"
½"x3½"
4"
END VIEW
ENLARGED
30"
SIDE VIEW

Plans for baby-chick feeder.

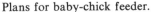

houses already described, depending on the size of the flock. In many instances it will be possible to rear enough pullets to fill both houses. Then enough can be culled out and sold during March or April to release one house for brooding again.

Brooder—The second major piece of equipment for rearing chicks is a brooder stove or some other means of keeping them warm. Many backyard poultry raisers starting 50 chicks or so use their basement or other room where a temperature of 65 to 70 degrees Fahrenheit can be maintained constantly. In such a room and for these small broods, a reasonably satisfactory brooder can be made of a cardboard box and suspending an infrared lamp above it for heat. You might use two just in case one burns out. A box about 30 by 30 inches with the lamp centered is satisfactory for starting about 50 chicks. In addition to this warm box, the chicks should have a pen, somewhat larger than the hover, into which they can run and in which the feed and water is placed. This also can be of cardboard. A curtain stretched across between the hover and the pen and extending down within an inch or two of the floor will retain the heat within the hover. It will not harm the chicks to run out into the cooler pen as long as they have a warm place to which they can go at will.

This is about the simplest type of hover and would not be recommended for use except for a small brood and then only in a warm room or for very late spring or summer brooding if used in an unheated building.

For brooding in cold weather or in unheated buildings, brooder stoves heated by electricity, coal, oil, wood, or gas can be purchased from any poultry equipment dealer. In addition to providing much more heat than the light-bulb arrangement, they also are equipped with thermostats which regulate the heat closely. For simplicity of operation and safety, electric brooders are highly recommended where electricity is available.

In determining what size of brooder to get (or how many chicks to place under a brooder), figure on seven square inches per chick under electric hovers. With other types, be sure to get a brooder with sufficient heating capacity for your house, then figure not more than three chicks per square foot for the first six weeks, with a maximum of 300 to 350 chicks in one brood. Other circumstances (the type of building, its insulation, section of the country, season of year, etc.) may affect the heating capacity of a brooder, but if in doubt, get a larger size.

Temperature Alarm—A very valuable, yet inexpensive, item of equipment is a temperature alarm. This involves a simple thermostat in the brooder house wired to an electric alarm bell in the dwelling house and operated by dry-cell batteries or by the regular electric-light circuit through the use of a transformer. The thermostat can be adjusted to allow a few degrees variation in the brooder-house temperature before it makes contact, closing the circuit and ringing the bell.

Usually the best location for the bell is in the bedroom, where it will serve to warn of an overheated or cold brooder house during the night. Such an arrangement has saved many a brood of chicks. One time, when I apparently failed to fasten the door latch securely, the wind blew the door open. But for the warning bell, I would have found a brood of frozen or smothered chicks next morning. In another instance, I was called out when a high wind plus an improper draft adjustment caused a coal stove to overheat. Here again the result would have been smothered chicks or even complete destruction of the house.

To reduce the fire hazard further, put an asbestos sheet or other fire-resistant material under the brooder.

Feeders and Fountains—Small feeders made of cardboard, metal, or wood to provide one inch of feeder space per chick, and water fountains also will be needed. The fountains can be ordinary quart Mason

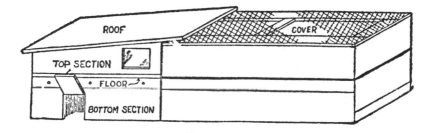

Small brooder and sunporch for 50 chicks or less, popular in the South. It has a 3-x-4-foot brooder unit, with metal floor and about 24 inches head room of weathertight construction. This compartment is heated with an ordinary kerosene kitchen lamp or electric light bulb. A 3-x-6-foot sun porch with wire or slatted floor is fitted to this brooder unit to give the chicks access to sunshine. They should be set up outdoors, especially in view of the fire hazard from kerosene lamps.

jars with special screw-on fountain bases which can be secured from any equipment dealer. There should be two of these fountains for each 100 chicks. Both the feeders and fountains will need to be exchanged for larger sizes as the chicks grow.

When 50 or more hens are kept, it will be almost essential to have a laying house and a brooder house in addition, of about the 10-by-12-foot size.

With two houses like this, it would be possible to raise two broods of chicks each year. When the pullets from the first brood are ready to replace the hens in the laying house, a second brood of chicks can be

BILL OF MATERIALS FOR 10-BY-10-FOOT RANGE SHELTER

Skids	2 pieces 2" × 10" × 12'
Floor Supports and End Studs	11 pieces 2" × 4" × 10'
Corner Studs	1 piece 2" × 6" × 10'
End Rafters and Side Studs	3 pieces 2" × 4" × 14'
Center Rafters	3 pieces 1" × 4" × 14'
Roof Nailing Strips	8 pieces 1" × 4" × 12'
Roost Supports	4 pieces 1" × 4" × 8'
Rear Door Frames	4 pieces 1" × 4" × 10'
Front Door and Trim around Rear Door	7 pieces 1" × 2" × 8'
Roosts	8 pieces 2" × 2" × 10'
Drop Siding—Side Walls	8 pieces 1" × 6" × 10'
Drop Siding—Gables and Rear Center Panel	10 pieces 1" × 6" × 8'
Rear Doors	1 piece 4' × 6' hard board
Roofing	12 pieces sheet steel 7 or structural insulation*
Ridge Roll	1 12' length copper-bearing, 28 gauge, 14" girth

Hardware

14 ft. 1" mesh, hexagonal poultry netting, 60" wide (16 gauge) for ends
20 ft. 1" × 2" welded wire fabric, 60" wide (14 or 12½ gauge) for floor
3 lbs. lead head 2" roofing nails
2 lbs. wire netting staples
2 pair 3" strap hinges for rear doors
2 lbs. 6d nails
2 lbs. 16d nails

*To use insulation board, space the four nailing strips evenly on rafters. Use the tongue and groove structural insulation sheathing which is 2' × 8' and ¾ inch thick. To make joints water-tight, apply roofing cement to upper side of tongue before joining. Add three gallons of liquid asphalt paint for roof to the bill of materials and substitute 1½" galvanized roofing nails for those specified above.

started in the brooder house, either to be held as layers or to be sold as broilers. Or, as mentioned before, enough pullets may be grown in one brood to fill both houses until the following spring.

Range Shelter—On farms using one or more brooder houses of approximately the 10-by-12-foot size, and rearing their birds on grass range, it is extremely helpful also to have a range shelter, for which plans are shown. Since pullets grow so fast, they become too crowded in the brooder house by the time they are eight or ten weeks old. If half of them can be moved into a range shelter, the whole brood will mature more evenly and with less mortality. A 10-by-10-foot range shelter, as shown, will provide roosting space for approximately 125 pullets, but, if desired, the shelter can be made 10-by-12-foot or larger.

Batteries and Cages—While the floor system usually is much more practical for the beginner, it is possible to raise chicks in wire trays or pens several tiers high, known as batteries. The principal advantage is that more chicks can be brooded in a given floor space.

In cold weather, most batteries must be used in a room which can be kept fairly warm. Individual heating units under thermostatic control or infrared lamps in each tray provide the additional heat necessary. Feeding and watering facilities are provided in troughs around the outside edge of the trays.

For broiler production, two or three sets of batteries usually are needed, one in which to start the chicks for four to six weeks, and other large batteries which may be heated or unheated in which to grow and finish out the broilers.

The growing batteries also can be used for rearing pullets which then are transferred to laying cages, with one to three hens in each cage. Laying cages usually are only one deck high but may be arranged in a variety of ways.

As mentioned earlier, laying cages are not really designed for small flocks. But if you can get a section of cages at reasonable cost, you might like to try them. For such use, they are well adapted for placement in a basement with a concrete floor and drain. Some handymen build their own batteries and cages after studying others.

Miscellaneous Equipment—Various items of general equipment also will be needed. Some special containers should be provided for feed storage. Such containers will be more convenient and cleaner, and there is less likelihood of attracting rats and mice than when the feed simply is kept in bags. These containers can be metal or fiber garbage cans, barrels, or bins. If several 100-pound bags of feed must be kept on hand, however, they should be stored on open racks in rooms which are rat- and mouseproof, with concrete floors and with the

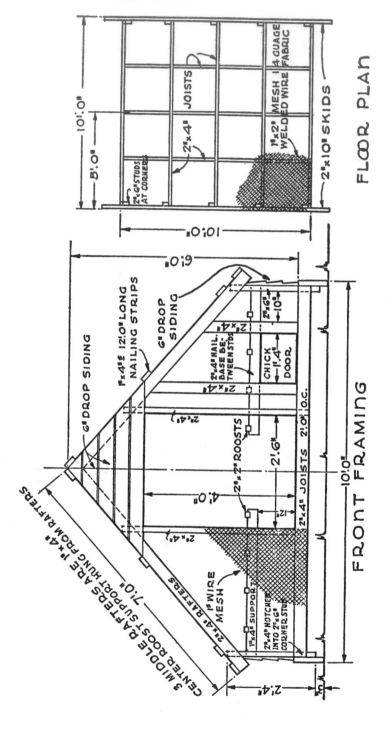

FLOOR PLAN

10'-0"

5'-0"

2"x4" JOISTS

2"x6"STUDS
AT CORNERS

1"x2" MESH 14 GUAGE
WELDED WIRE FABRIC

2"x10" SKIDS

10'-0"

FRONT FRAMING

6'-0"

1"x4" 12'0" LONG
NAILING STRIPS

6" DROP SIDING

6" DROP SIDING

2"x4" NAIL
BASE BE-
TWEEN STDS

2"x4"

CHICK
1'-4"
DOOR

2"x6"
10"

2"x4"

2"x4"

2"x2" ROOSTS

2'-6"

2"x4" JOISTS 2'-0" O.C.

4'-0"

12"

12"

10'-0"

3 MIDDLE RAFTERS ARE 1"x4"
CENTER ROOST SUPPORT HUNG FROM RAFTERS
7'-0"

2"x4" RAFTERS

1" WIRE
MESH

1"x4" SUPPORT

2"x4" NOTCHED
INTO 2"x6"
CORNER STUD

2'-4"

4"

RANGE SHELTER
(Bill of materials on page 40)

sides and ceiling covered with sheet steel or hardware cloth. Three rats can eat or destroy as much feed in a year's time as two hens will eat.

Small items which will be needed are half-bushel measures or pails which can be used to carry feed, a feed scoop, an oil pail or coal bucket, if those fuels are used for brooding, a scraper for cleaning the floor (a hoe may serve in a small house), a sprayer for disinfecting, and a shovel for handling the litter and droppings.

The actual management of the chicks and hens will be covered in the next two chapters.

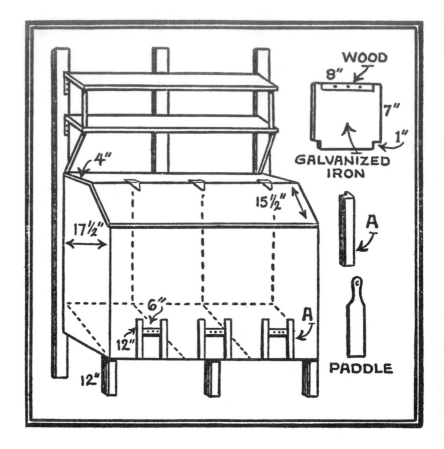

A bin like this is a convenience in storing feed and other supplies. It may have as many divisions as wanted or as space permits. This one has three. The sliding gates are made of galvanized iron, and the bottom of the bin is lined with galvanized iron. The bottom of the bin slopes toward the sliding gates, so the feed will flow out freely. The bin is high enough from the floor to permit pails to slide under. Small coal hods make excellent pails to fill feeders. On the shelves are kept tools, nails, screws, etc., in glass containers, remedies, and disinfectants.

4
Brooding and Rearing Chicks

Now that chicks have been ordered and the necessary housing and equipment arranged for, the next step is to be prepared for the arrival of the chicks and to know how to take care of them.

Successful chick brooding is not particularly difficult, but it does require close observance of a few tried and tested principles. If you visit very many people who raise chickens, you probably will see so many different arrangements of houses and brooders and hear of so many different kinds of feed and ways of feeding that you may feel there is no uniformity in brooding practices. Underlying the methods used by all poultry raisers who are successful year after year, however, are at least three essentials. These are warmth for comfort, feed and water for good growth, and sanitary surroundings to prevent disease.

GETTING READY FOR THE CHICKS
When arrangements are made with a hatcheryman to supply chicks, he usually promises delivery of them on a certain date, or very close to it. Many hatcherymen and dealers follow the practice of sending a

postal card to chick buyers two or three days ahead of the shipment of chicks to warn of their coming.

And it is important to be ready for the chicks, for they are babies, and the sooner they can be placed in warm quarters and given their first feeding, the better the start they will make.

Not only because of their interest, but also because of their value in guiding future operations, careful brooding records should be kept. These should include all items of expense (and income, if any) as well as the date and cause (if known) of all chick losses.

PREPARING THE HOUSE

If a new house is being used, it probably will require no special preparation except to be sure that it is completed in ample time for the chicks. If an old building, especially one which has had chickens it it previously, is to be used for brooding the chicks, then it needs to be thoroughly cleaned and disinfected. The ceiling, walls, and floor should have all the dust and dirt swept out. If dirt is caked on the floor, it should be scraped loose with a hoe, shovel, or other scraper. When the loose dirt has been taken out, soak and scrub the lower walls and floor, then apply a good disinfectant according to the manufacturer's directions. Allow time for the house to dry throughly.

The reason for this thorough cleaning is that the germs of several of the more serious poultry diseases may live for several months in the dirt and manure of a poultry house or the soil around it and be there ready to infect a new brood if the proper sanitation measures are not taken.

If the house is one in which the chickens will be raised to maturity, or in which laying hens will be kept later on (as contrasted with a temporary pen in a basement, garage, etc.), it would be wise to paint the lower walls, the roosts, nests, and the wall areas where these pieces of equipment join the walls, with a wood-preserving material, such as carbolineum. This will keep mites, one of the most troublesome parasites of chickens, out of the house for at least a year. There also are special mite-killing sprays and mixtures available at your hatchery, dealer, or drugstore. The mite-repellent material should be painted on several days before the chicks are put in the house; so that it will be thoroughly dry before they come in contact with it.

If an old building is used, it should be checked to be sure that it does not leak and that all cracks and openings other than the doors, windows, and ventilators, are closed to prevent drafts and also to prevent the entrance of rodents such as rats.

LOCATING THE BROODER HOUSE

When the amount of land available is limited, there may not be much choice as to the location for the brooder house, but on the average farm this should be a very important consideration.

Growing chicks should never be allowed to run on the same ground where the older chickens run or where chickens have ranged for the past few years. On most farms this will mean that the brooder house cannot be located close to the laying house or in the barnyard. An ideal location is a good sloping grass-sod or alfalfa field where no chickens have ranged or no poultry droppings have been scattered for at least two years and far enough away that there will be no opportunity for the chicks to come in contact with the older birds. An orchard makes a fair location for a brooder house because of the shade available, or the house may be set near the edge of a cornfield into which the chicks may run for shade. Of course, they should not be allowed in a cornfield until the corn is so high that they can no longer eat it.

After the house is cleaned is the time to move it to this new location, and not before. In this way, none of the dirt and filth from previous broods of chicks will be taken to the new location. For this reason, a good many poultry raisers plan to clean their brooder house in the fall and set it up on low blocks so that it can be pulled to the new location with a tractor or team of horses some time during the winter when the ground is frozen.

This requirement for clean ground means that it will be necessary to have three separate fields or range locations available where the brooder house can be located, using each one for only one year at a time.

SETTING UP THE BROODER

As soon as the building is ready, the second step is to set up the brooder. If this is just a small cardboard affair for a few chicks, it will take little longer than the time necessary to cut the cardboard and insert a light bulb. The manufactured brooders will take a little longer to set up, especially if they are new and must be assembled, and if you have not had previous experience with one. In this case, it is especially important to set it up several days ahead of the time the chicks are expected and to follow carefully the manufacturer's directions. If the directions are observed, there is not much chance of making a mistake in setting up a manufactured brooder. But even with the simplest brooding equipment, it pays to operate it for a few days to make sure it is doing the job right. It's much better to get all the adjustments made before the chicks arrive. I've been amazed at how often this is neglected.

It usually is more satisfactory to place the brooder somewhat nearer to one wall, rather than putting it in the exact center of the brooder house. For this reason, when broods as large as two or three hundred chicks are being raised, a house around 12 by 12 feet, or somewhat larger than the customary 10-by-12-foot brooder house, is preferable. The reason for putting the brooder nearer one side is to provide the chicks with a greater range in temperature, and with an opportunity to get farther away from the heat, particularly when coal, oil, wood, or gas brooders are used. This is not so important with electric brooders, for they do not provide much heat outside the hover anyway.

Under the base of coal, oil, or wood brooders, it adds to safety if a sheet of metal or a ring of sand is used. This helps to protect the floor in case, by chance, the brooder should become overheated.

After the brooder has been installed, it should be tested to make sure that it provides plenty of heat and operates satisfactorily, particularly the thermostat, which should keep the stove quite accurately at the temperature for which it is set. In making this test, keep in mind that a temperature of 90 to 95 degrees Fahrenheit will be wanted where the chicks sleep. Under an electric brooder, or a cardboard, homemade arrangement, this will be right under the hover. In other types it will be about six inches out from the edge of the hover and at the floor. Don't make the mistake of hanging the brooder thermometer high on the wall, for the temperature at the floor will be several degrees cooler. In a homemade brooder which has no way to regulate the amount of heat, it must be kept in mind that the chicks will provide some heat, but it is better to have a surplus to take care of weather changes, than too little, for the chicks can move out from under the brooder if they get too warm.

Manufactured brooders, as a rule, have thermostats which can be adjusted to maintain an accurate temperature during moderate weather changes. In severe changes, some manual changes in the amount of fuel will be needed, particularly in coal and oil brooders.

Other items which will help to make the operation of a brooder stove safer and more satisfactory will be a draft equalizer, which is inserted in the pipe a short distance above the stove; a roof saddle of metal which holds the pipe at least three inches away from any wood or other inflammable roof material; and sometimes, a revolving hood on the pipe where down drafts occur. Sometimes there appears to be insufficient draft in a stove and extra lengths of pipe are needed to increase the height. There may also be difficulty in getting sufficient draft if the brooder house happens to be located too close to a barn or other higher building which shelters it from the wind. Of course, these items, as well as the draft problem, are not involved when electric or gas brooders are used.

The brooder stove should be operated long enough to be sure that it is operating properly. In cold weather, it may be necessary to operate it for two or three days before the chicks arrive in order to get the house thoroughly warm and dry.

LITTER

Once the brooder stove has been set up and thoroughly tested, place about two inches of litter of the floor. There is a great variety of litters available, some of them only locally. Among the litter materials which may be purchased in most parts of the courtry are shredded sugarcane fiber, peat moss, treated cottonseed hulls, oat hulls, softwood shavings, and several types of mineral litters. Sometimes materials on the farm such as ground corncobs, chopped straw, or alfalfa or clover leaves, can be used. Any litter used should be free of molds. Its purpose is to absorb the moisture from the droppings and to provide a bed for the chicks. Therefore, it must be an absorptive material. Since straw is quite poor in this regard, it cannot be very highly recommended as litter, although it is used fairly frequently because of its ready availability. Even farmers who have straw available, however, usually would be better off to buy a more absorptive material.

In a very small brood of chicks started in a basement or other temporary quarters, the litter probably should not be more than one or two inches deep and should be changed every one to two weeks.

In a larger brood in a regular brooder house, however, it is better to use what is known as a deep litter. In this case, it is helpful, but not essential, to have about an inch of clean, coarse sand over the floor as a base for the litter. Then spread about two inches of litter over the sand, stirring it with a fork or rake every day or two. Each week add a thin layer of new litter until it is about four inches deep by the time the chicks are five weeks old. A deep, dry litter built up in this way can be used throughout the brooding season, as long as there are no outbreaks of disease. Such a litter helps to prevent disease outbreaks and saves a great deal of labor and time.

Some poultry raisers spread several thicknesses of newspapers over the litter for the first three or four days until the chicks learn to eat. A layer of papers is removed and burned each day. The use of newspapers in this way is not necessary, however, if plenty of feeders are provided from the start. In fact, the use of slick papers may make it difficult for the chicks to stand, even to the point of causing some of them to become spraddle-legged.

But whether a shallow or deep layer of litter is used, the main thing is to keep it dry. If a part of it becomes wet around the water fountains or if rain should blow in, the wet litter should be replaced with dry material immediately.

CHICK GUARD

In continuing preparations for the chicks, the next step is to make a pen around the hover with corrugated cardboard, wire netting covered with cloth, or some similar arrangement. This is known as a chick guard. Special chicks guards of corrugated cardboard can be purchased for this purpose from hatcherymen and dealers. With most types of brooders, the chick guard can be set up in the form of a ring eighteen inches to two feet away from the edge of the hover. Its purpose is to keep the chicks from wandering too far away from the source of heat for the first few days. Sometimes in a basement or backyard project, it will be better simply to make a little pen in front of the hover. This chick guard can be moved a few inches farther away from the hover each day and taken away entirely by the end of the first week, unless the weather is extremely cold.

FEEDERS AND FOUNTAINS

Inside the chick guard and radiating away from the stove like the spokes in a wheel set the small chick feeders. Also set several water fountains around the brooder according to the size of house and number of chicks being brooded, as recommended in Chapter 3.

Fill the feeders moderately full of chick-starting mash, and on the day the chicks arrive, fill the fountains with water from which the chill has been removed.

Extra feed can be kept in the brooder house, either in the original bag sitting outside the chick guard or in a covered container, such as a barrel or garbage pail. Since feeders and fountains usually will be filled only once a day, however, this isn't necessary, and the feed may be kept in some other building.

In addition to small trough feeders, it will be a good idea to put down a few pieces of cardboard or egg case flats on which a little feed can be sprinkled. If these are left in the house for a day or two the chicks will learn to eat more quickly and there will be little danger of their picking up litter. It also will help to keep the chicks and litter dry if the fountains are set on pieces of board which provide them with a solid base and keep them up out of the litter.

This may seem like a lot of emphasis upon getting ready for the chicks, but it will be found that thorough preparation does much to

Ideal brooding arrangement for chicks when they are started. Fountains are on egg case flats. Feed is sprinkled on flats to make it easy for chicks to begin eating.

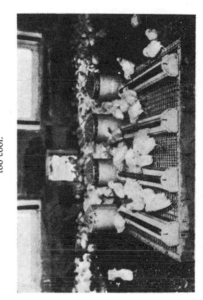

When temperature is right, this is way chicks settle down around brooder stove. If farther away, they are too warm; if closer, they are too cool.

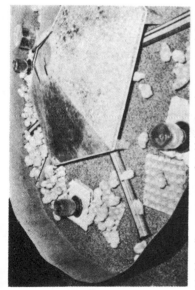

When chicks are four or five weeks old, they can be taught to roost by use of sloping roosts like these. Front edge can be gradually lifted until roost is level.

Arranging feeders and fountains on a wire covered platform helps to keep litter dry.

When brooder houses are far from the water supply, a barrel waterer with automatic valve control may be used. Scrub out with disinfectant about once a week.

Add fresh feed each day instead of filling feeders to capacity. Stir feed by hand or stick occasionally to stimulate consumption.

Range shelter located on alfalfa range. Corn field provides shade.

On some farms, thousands of hens are kept in batteries.

insure success. If everything is in readiness to give the chicks a good start, the actual brooding frequently seems ridiculously simple, whereas if the chicks become chilled or if they are starved for the first day or so, it seems that difficulties usually multiply from then on.

I don't think I fully appreciated the importance of thorough preparation until I went out with a hatcheryman to deliver several broods of chicks. We found brooder houses in all degrees of readiness from those carefully arranged in every detail, warm and dry, and with feed and water ready, to those like the one of the man who hadn't "got to it yet, but I'll just set them in the kitchen until I get the brooder house fixed up this afternoon."

It's from the latter type of chick buyer that the majority of complaints and stories of "bad luck" come, although misfortune occasionally overtakes the most careful.

WHEN THE CHICKS ARRIVE

You are now ready for the day when the chicks will be delivered or when you will go for them, full of anticipation and hope for the new enterprise ahead. This day holds high interest, even for experienced poultry raisers, for there always is a thrill in starting a new brood, with their prospect of providing food or profit within a few short weeks.

In bringing them home, protect the boxes from strong winds and exposure to cold. As soon as they are brought home, they can be taken directly to the brooder house if it is warm and ready. Otherwise, they can be set in the kitchen or other room where the temperature is around 70 to 80 degrees Fahrenheit.

If the chicks arrive late in the afternoon or at night, it probably would be better to leave them in the chick boxes overnight. If they arrive earlier in the day, they can be placed under the hover immediately.

As they are taken from the chick boxes, count them and place them well under the hover. Some poultry raisers follow the custom of dipping the beak of each chick in the warmed water before putting them under the hover. While this isn't essential at all, it certainly does no harm and may help to refresh chicks which have traveled some distance.

Always have the feed and water ready for them when they are placed in the house. Within a very few minutes a few of them will be picking at the feed on the cardboard and in the feeders and will be tasting the water. If there is no feed ready, they will start picking at the litter which, in most instances, will cause indigestion and some death loss if very much of it is eaten.

BROODING MANAGEMENT

The first three or four nights are important in establishing correct sleeping habits in the chicks. If the temperature is about right and the house is free of drafts, the chicks will tend to settle down in a ring about six inches or so from the edge of the hover (or spread out evenly under an electric hover). A starting temperature of around 90 to 95 degrees Fahrenheit usually will produce this result. If they are too hot, the chicks will tend to spread out their wings, pant, and try to get away from the heat. If they are too cool, they will tend to huddle together and make their discomfort known by rather shrill chirping. The worst of it is they are just as likely to huddle in the coldest corner of the house as next to the brooder, and if they are not dispersed, they will continue to huddle and crowd until some are smothered to death. So, about dusk each evening, it is important to make sure they settle down properly around the hover, although these symptoms of being too hot or too cold may be observed at any time during the day. Check their arrangement again at your bedtime. People who don't use a brooder alarm usually get up to look at the chicks two or three times a night for the first week or two. I've known poultrymen who even slept right in the brooder house for a few nights.

Another advantage of the electric hover is that there usually is a small light burning under it which attracts the chicks to congregate under the hover when it becomes dark in the brooder house.

This tendency of chicks to huddle together and crowd is another reason for using the circular chick guard, which keeps them out of corners. Even after the chick guard is removed, many poultry raisers round out the corners of square brooder houses with cardboard, metal, or other material to keep the chicks from piling back into corners.

The temperature can be reduced at a rate of about five degrees each week until it is down to around 70 degrees Fahrenheit. Even more important, however, is to observe the action of the chicks and regulate the temperature accordingly. By the way they use the brooder, as described in the preceding paragraph, it is possible to tell whether they are too warm, too cold, or about right.

In spring broods of chicks started after the middle of March, it is seldom necessary to provide heat for more than about six weeks. In extremely cold or damp weather, however, it may be necessary to provide a little heat longer than that, especially at night, to prevent crowding and piling and to keep the house dry. Late spring broods may need heat only a week or two unless the nights are unusually cool.

In a lamp-bulb type of brooder, the heat adjustment can be made by using a smaller size of bulb or by raising the hover to allow more ventilation. In the larger standard brooders, the adjustment is made by changing the thermostat setting to keep the temperature lower. Even with the larger electric hovers, however, it may be more desirable to raise the hover as the chicks grow than to make all the adjust-

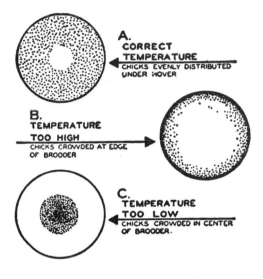

Chart showing how chicks distribute themselves under correct and incorrect temperature conditions under electric hovers. Adjust the temperature until the chicks spread out evenly at night as in "A," with the attraction light turned off. When the chicks grow older and begin gathering toward the edge of the hover, as in "B," it may be simpler to raise the hover slightly rather than adjusting the thermostat. (*University of Delaware*)

ments with the thermostat. The chicks can be provided with more ventilation also through the windows or other ventilators.

The draft and fuel supply of oil, coal, and wood stoves should be checked occasionally during the day. Except in extremely severe weather, the oil tank will need refilling only once a day. Coal and wood stoves should have attention twice a day. When the ashes are removed, be extremely careful that live coals are not left in the litter. It probably is best to clean out ashes and add coal or wood at about 4 P.M. so that the fire will be burning well when the outside temperature drops. If this is delayed until late, the new fuel may smother the fire until it may not start up quickly enough to keep the house at the proper temperature.

Anthracite is universally recommended for coal stoves. Soft coal can be used in case of necessity, but it will require frequent attention and the soot usually will clog the stovepipe from time to time. When this happens, the pipe will have to removed and cleaned.

Brooder stoves also need close attention as the outside temperature changes. A house that is just right at 8 A.M. may be entirely too warm by noon if the sun comes out hot and the windows are left closed. Then the reverse will be true in the afternoon. If the brooder stove is adjusted to maintain the proper temperature during the night, control the day temperature by opening windows. If the windows tilt in at the top or are covered with muslin, there usually will be no disagreeable drafts.

FEEDING

As far as feeding methods go, it is best to follow the recommendations of the company which manufactures the feed used, for some feeds are designed to be fed with grain, while others are not. An excellent system, preferred because it is simpler and saves work, is to have the starting mash before the chicks as already explained, and to keep it before them in hoppers all of the time for the first six to twelve weeks. Along with this they may have a little fine chick grit or sand, which may be in a separate container or sprinkled lightly over the mash. With this method, the hoppers can be filled once a day, taking care not to fill them too full so that the chicks "bill" out the feed and waste it.

Feed also may be bought in the form of pellets or crumbles. These may cost a little more than the mash but they seem to be more palatable to the chicks and there is less feed waste when they are used.

Most starter feeds will contain a coccidiostat—a drug to prevent coccidiosis, one of the most common diseases during the growing period. Be sure to read and follow the directions carefully. The purpose of the coccidiostat is to help the chicks develop an immunity to the disease by the time they are a couple of months old. Keep fresh feed available but don't waste it by overfilling the feeders.

Water fountains should be cleaned and refilled each day also. Wash them thoroughly with a good disinfectant about once a week.

Continue the starting mash for six to twelve weeks according to the maker's recommendations. Usually some chick grain can be fed, beginning at about four weeks and gradually increased in quantity. At first this can be sprinkled lightly on top of the mash and later fed in separate hoppers.

At the six- to twelve-week age, whenever recommended, the pullet chicks which are to be saved as layers are switched to what is known as a growing mash, which is lower in protein and, therefore, does not tend to force such rapid growth of the birds. They may have both growing mash and grain before them in separate hoppers all of the time. The grain may consist of a mixture of cracked corn and wheat, with whole oats fed separately, or other grains, such as barley and the sorghum grains, may be substituted as available. Here, again, the hatcheryman or feed dealer will be able to suggest the method to follow with the feed he sells.

Chicks which are to be grown for meat purposes only can be started on either starting mash or a special broiler mash made by practically all feed companies. This broiler mash (or the starter mash if broiler mash is not available) can be fed straight through until the birds are ready to sell or kill at a weight of from three to four pounds. These feeds produce very rapid growth, and while they are more expensive than growing mash, they usually will be more economical for meat production. Grain or pellets should be fed according to directions with the ration used.

In broods having both pullets and cockerels, and in which the pullets are to be saved for laying, the cockerels can be separated out at about six weeks of age and continued on a broiler mash as for meat birds. In fact, commercial broiler growers find that it pays to grow the sexes separately even when both the cockerels and pullets are being raised for meat.

It is possible to mix poultry feeds at home, and good formulas are available at agricultural colleges and other sources, but this usually is not economical or satisfactory for people growing chickens in small numbers, for it is too difficult to gather the numerous ingredients needed and mix them each time a fresh supply of feed is required. A chick eats only a thimbleful of feed daily at first, and from that small quantity it must get protein, carbohydrates, fat, vitamins, and minerals in the right proportions to build bone, muscle, and feathers.

The large feed companies follow the findings of all of the agricultural colleges and, in addition, most of them have large experimental farms and laboratories of their own where they are constantly developing and testing new feeds. They are therefore in a position to supply exceedingly satisfactory products. Furthermore, most dealers and hatcherymen will sell feed in as small quantities as desired.

It is not wise to buy feed in too large quantities. Only under unusual circumstances should mash be bought in quantities that will last more than a month or two ahead, and many poultry raisers like to get it once every few weeks in order to have it as fresh as possible. To provide a guide as to the amount of feed required, the following figures may be used. Leghorn-type chicks will eat about .4 pound (40 pounds per 100 chicks) in the first 2 weeks; the accumulated total at later ages will be about 1.1 pounds (110 pounds per 100 pullets) by 4 weeks of age; 3.25 pounds (325 pounds per 100 pullets) by 8 weeks; 7.0 pounds by 12 weeks; 11.0 pounds by 16 weeks; and about 15.0 pounds per pullet by 20 weeks of age, when they may begin laying.

These amounts will vary somewhat according to the strain of chicks, the method of feeding, and the amount of feed wasted.

As a guide to how fast your pullets may grow, they can be expected to average about 1 pound each by 6 weeks of age; 2 pounds by 12 to 14 weeks; and about 3 pounds by 20 weeks. Again, the exact weights will vary by strain and feeding methods. There also will be variation, of course, in the weight of the individual birds.

The heavier breeds or strains, such as the brown-egg strains, will weigh more at each age, and, of course, will eat more in proportion to their weight.

Good poultrymen like to bring their pullets to the laying stage without excess fat. They feel that such pullets won't begin laying quite so soon but that the birds will be a little larger, and their first eggs will be larger, when they finally begin to lay. To accomplish this, feed consumption is restricted moderately during the later weeks of growth. Such a program requires adequate equipment and management skill, however, and beginners probably should not attempt it. It is mentioned here only because you may read or hear of it and be tempted to try it before you fully understand the program.

If you buy one of the well-known strains of chicks, the breeder probably has a specific management program which he recommends for his chicks. You will do well to study his program and follow it closely. After all, he knows his stock, and he is anxious for it to do well for you.

When the chicks are eating well out of low feeders, remove the cardboards which were suggested earlier. As the chicks grow, change to larger feeders and raise them gradually. Less feed will be "billed out" and wasted when this is done.

If you are using hanging feeders, they can be set on the floor for the first week or two. When the chicks have learned to eat from them, raise them gradually.

Don't make sudden complete changes from one type of feeder or waterer to another. Keep both the old and new types in use for a few days to allow the chicks to become fully familiar with the new equipment.

In fact, this suggestion of gradual change is important in all poultry management. Chickens are very much creatures of habit and should not be subjected to sudden changes in feed, equipment, or routine.

You may not think of water as feed but it is extremely important in good chick and pullet care. Chickens of all ages should have water constantly where they will never have to walk more than 10 to 15 feet for it.

The attitudes of chickens toward water are not too different from your own. They like it best when the water temperature is between 50 and 70 degrees Fahrenheit. They drink more in hot weather. They drink more when they are working harder. An egg is about 65 percent water, so water consumption may increase as much as 50 percent as the birds near full egg production.

As you increase the feeder space, be sure to increase the drinking space; they drink more as they eat more.

Healthier pullets will be raised and considerable feed can be saved if they can be provided with ample green feed. The main thing in providing green feed is to have it young and tender. Chickens cannot digest coarse or dry grass, and it is likely to cause them to become cropbound.

If the chicks must be raised in a bare lot or on a sun porch, they can be given freshly cut lawn clippings or the fresh tops and leaves of such garden vegetables as carrots, beets, cabbage, and kale. A small patch of rape in one corner of the garden would provide considerable green feed if there is none other available.

Where the pullets are grown on range, there should be a good sod of blue grass or such a range crop as alfalfa or clover. It will be better for the chickens if it is kept mowed rather close to keep it fresh and tender. When the range is managed especially for chickens, it is recommended that it be mowed every week or ten days.

Chickens have no teeth and their feed is ground in the gizzard. To aid in this grinding process, grit usually is fed throughout the life of the chicken. A suitable grit can be purchased from hatcherymen and feed dealers or hard, sharp gravel may serve. The fine chick grit can be sprinkled lightly on top of the mash at first, then a constant supply can be kept in a small hopper or a compartment of the regular mash hopper before the birds all of the time.

In addition, pullets will need a source of lime, not only for bone formation, but for making eggshells when they begin laying. Therefore, crushed oyster shells, ground limestone, or some other source of lime should be provided for the pullets constantly after they are three or four months old.

GENERAL MANAGEMENT

If the weather is clear, the chicks can be allowed to run outside when they are two or three weeks old, or even younger, late in the spring. Even when there is plenty of ground available, however, it is best to keep them confined to a rather small pen for the first few days.

It is extremely important in avoiding disease that the young chicks do not run on ground where other chickens have ranged for at least two years, and that they do not come in contact with adult birds. Even on clean ground it is a sound practice to move the house to a new location often enough to keep the ground from becoming bare around it. Moving it a few rods will be sufficient, for pullets will not range so very far on good range, especially if well fed.

If several houses are on the same range, the number of growing chickens per acre may range from 200 to 400 or even higher, depending on the crop used and how well established it is.

When it is impossible to provide a change of ground each year, it eventually will become necessary to grow the chickens in confinement, either in batteries or with the use of sun porches attached to the brooder house. The sun porch can be about the same size as the brooder house and enclosed with either wire or slats. The floor can be a welded wire fabric of about 1-by-1-inch or 1-by-2-inch mesh or hardware screen of about ¾-inch mesh, while the sides and top can be ordinary poultry netting. If wooden slats are used 1-by-1-inch slats for the floor and lath for the sides and top are satisfactory.

It will be necessary to double the feeder space (to about 2 linear inches per chick) at 2 or 3 weeks; increase it to 3 inches per chick at about 6 weeks; and to 4 inches at 12 weeks of age. Increase the water fountain capacity at the same time—shifting to two 3-gallon fountains at 2 or 3 weeks, then two 5-gallon fountains at about 8 weeks.

As long as the feed hoppers and fountains must be kept in the brooder house, it will help to keep the litter dry and help to prevent waste if they are set on low platforms covered with wire or slats. Even when they are set outside on the ground, it will be helpful to continue use of these platforms, or else to move the feeders and fountains to a new location every two or three days, or both.

For range use, larger covered feeders, like the one illustrated, will be preferable. Use three five-foot feeders for each 125 pullets. At first, two for mash and one for grain will be satisfactory, but the proportion of grain eaten will increase until the ratio can be reversed at about three months of age. The use of a barrel-waterer with automatic valve also will be a great convenience on range. If water under pressure is

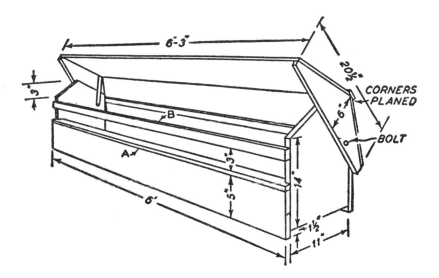

This style of range feeder gives good protection to the feed. Note that "A" is a strip of 1½-x-⅜-inch material to prevent the feed from being picked out of the feeder. "B" is a strip of 1½-x-1-inch material which can be raised or lowered to suit the size of the birds.

available, it will be a great labor-saver to pipe it directly to the range and use float fountains when several hundred birds are being reared.

It is desirable to install roosts by the time the chicks are around six weeks old. These can be arranged so that they are about a foot high at the rear wall, and slope to the floor at front. As the chicks learn to use them, raise them in front until they are level. Use a board or wire along the front to keep the chicks from going under them.

RANGE CARE

As mentioned in Chapter 3, chicks can be started the first year in the same house which later will be used for the laying hens. In the second year, however, this house will not be available for rearing the chicks. Frequently they can be started in temporary quarters, such as a basement or garage, as already mentioned, but they will need different quarters to grow them to maturity. On a farm particularly, and else-where if ground is available, the best practice is to have a range shelter to which the pullets can be taken when they are around eight or ten weeks old, depending on how early in the spring they were started. A range shelter like the one for which plans are given in Chapter 3 is excellent for growing pullets, as it provides plenty of ventilation dur-ing the summer, yet protects the pullets from storms and from preda-tory animals. For small numbers of pullets, the shelter does not have to be constructed as heavily as shown in the plan. A suitable small shelter frequently can be made of scrap materials for the framing and roof, with wire netting to cover the sides.

If the pullets are to be vaccinated for fowl pox or infectious laryn-gotracheitis, this needs to be done when they are between eight and sixteen weeks of age. Frequently it can be done when the chicks are moved to the range house, and, in this way, an extra handling can be avoided.

It is doubtful whether the average small backyard flock should be vaccinated, but it is more likely to be worthwhile in farm flocks. In deciding whether to vaccinate, consider whether these diseases have appeared in your own flock before or whether they are prevalent in the community. If you have not had either fowl pox or laryngotra-cheitis in your own birds and do not know of any other flocks which have suffered from them, it should not be necessary to vaccinate. Vaccination is positive in preventing these diseases, however, so if they are prevalent in the community, do not neglect it. The methods are outlined in Chapter 6.

At about four or five months of age, the comb, face, and wattles of a few pullets will redden up and the birds will lose some of their "gangly" appearance and develop more of a well-rounded, mature body shape. This means that they are about ready to begin laying eggs and some changes in management can be made soon. These will be covered in the next chapter on managing a laying flock.

MEAT PRODUCTION

As mentioned in Chapter 2, an entirely different type of chick is used for meat production—crosses which develop meaty breasts and legs. Birds with light-colored feathers are preferred because the carcasses make a better appearance.

In all likelihood you will be growing only a small brood of meat birds. For one thing, if you dress more than a few hundred birds, you must comply with state and/or federal poultry-inspection regulations which are strict in requiring specific standards in facilities and sanitation. You might, however, get them custom dressed in an inspected plant.

It definitely is not worthwhile to grow small broods of broilers with the expectation of selling the live birds to a commercial poultry dressing plant. As mentioned earlier, broiler growing is now a large-scale operation with very narrow margins of profit per bird.

But if you do wish to grow and dress out some meat birds, the brooding is done in exactly the same manner as for pullets. The feed used is specially formulated to produce fast growth. If you are in an area where few broilers are grown you may not be able to buy broiler feed. In that event, you may use the starting feeds used for pullets, continuing it for the entire growing period.

Broilers grow rapidly, reaching three or four pounds in six to eight weeks. So be sure to allow about one square foot of floor space per bird, and increase feeding and drinking space more rapidly than for pullets.

Most broiler growers provide light in the brooder house 24 hours a day throughout the entire growing period. One 60-watt bulb for each 200 square feet of floor space is sufficient.

For home use, you might like to consider growing some meat birds as roasters or capons. This just means growing the broiler chicks to a larger size—at least five pounds but usually considerably heavier.

Roasters are fed very much like pullets, beginning with the broiler feed or starting mash then switching to a finishing or growing mash and grain.

Allow about three square feet of floor space per bird if grown in confinement; however, roasters do well on range. If kept confined for more than 20 weeks, increase the floor space to four square feet per bird. These heavy birds will cost more per pound to grow but are delicious!

Of all classes of poultry, probably none exceed the capon in fine quality and flavor. A capon is simply a male with the sex organs removed, the same as a steer in cattle.

While the operation is not particularly difficult, it does require some practice to become proficient. For a small flock it might be better to try to find someone who will do it for a few cents per bird. Sometimes a hatcheryman or one of his workmen, a high-school vocational-agriculture teacher, or some of his students may be willing to do it on a custom basis.

If you are interested in learning to perform the operation, however, suitable sets of instruments with complete instructions for their use can be purchased from most of the general poultry equipment companies.

Only the heavy breeds are caponized as a rule. If you do happen to have a few Leghorn-type males, they could be caponized for practice and will make good small capons.

The best time for the operation is just after the sexual organs start to develop, as indicated by the reddening of the head and comb. This usually will be when they are four to six weeks old.

Caponize only good, strong, healthy birds, for weaklings will not make satisfactory recovery and growth.

Withhold feed and water from the cockerels to be caponized for 12 to 18 hours. The incision is made between the last two ribs and about one inch from the backbone. Detailed instructions for making the incision and removing the testicle on each side will be provided with the particular instruments which you buy. No anesthetic is needed and the cockerels recover rather quickly if they are provided with a moist mash for food, plenty of drinking water, and shade for two or three days. Air puffs may develop on some of the capons during the following week or ten days after the operation and these can be relieved by puncturing the skin with a needle or sharp pointed knife.

They are fed and managed then like any other meat bird, giving them plenty of range if possible, not only for exercise, but in order to provide green feed. Capons should be grown to heavy weight to make them worthwhile, at least 4 or 5 pounds in the case of Leghorns; 6 to 8 pounds in the case of the American medium-size breeds; at least 8 to 12 pounds in the case of the very heavy breeds, such as Jersey Giants. Not only do capons provide excellent meat for home use, but they will usually bring a premium of a few cents per pound on the market, frequently equalling or exceeding turkeys in price.

BATTERIES

The use of battery brooders, which are in the form of trays several tiers high, to start chicks makes it possible to start a larger number in a room with relatively small floor space and also to economize on fuel.

Numerous types of battery brooders are available, but in most instances it will be necessary to provide a room with a temperature of at least 70 degrees Fahrenheit, while individual electric heaters in each tray provide the necessary heat.

The dropping pans should be cleaned every day, and the batteries thoroughly cleaned and disinfected between broods.

The feeding and other management of chicks in batteries is practically the same as that for chicks started on the floor. The main requirement is that the chicks be given ample space.

The following table shows how to determine the chick capacity of battery brooders. These figures are conservative and perhaps it woulc seem that more chicks could be put in the batteries than is suggested here. One of the most important things which poultry raisers need to keep in mind, however, is that chickens ought never to be overcrowded. It always is better to give them more space than seems necessary, rather than to crowd them. Crowding will lead to slower growth and frequently also will lead to more serious difficulties in the form of feather picking and similar vices, as well as increasing the likelihood of disease outbreaks.

Many times the chicks are started in batteries for three or four weeks, then transferred to a brooder house. However, broilers can be reared to market age and pullets to maturity in batteries by providing frequent increases in space. Most of the battery manufacturers have excellent booklets detailing the program to be followed.

BATTERY BROODER CAPACITY

Age of Chicks Days	Floor Area for Each Chick Sq. In.
7	10
14	12
21	15
28	20
35	25
42	30
56	37
63	45

5
Managing the Laying Flock

In strains bred for high egg production, you may find the first egg when the pullets are around four or five months of age, or even a little earlier in the case of Leghorns. The main portion of the flock, however, ordinarily will not begin laying until it is at least six months of age.

HOUSING

If the pullets are grown on range or elsewhere away from the laying house, it will be well to plan to transfer them to the laying house within a short time after the first birds begin to lay. The following suggestions also are applicable if ready-to-lay pullets are purchased from another poultryman.

As pointed out in Chapter 3, Leghorns should have at least 3 to 3½ square feet of floor space, and heavier breeds about 4 square feet in the laying house. Like the brooder house, the laying house should be prepared by thoroughly cleaning, scrubbing, and disinfecting it and the equipment in it, unless it is all completely new. Likewise, have the house ready when the pullets are brought in by having litter on the floor (the same kind and amount as recommended for the brooder house in Chapter 4), feed, grit, and lime material in the feeders, water in the fountains, and suitable nests at the rate of about one nest for every five or six birds, or else a tunnel nest. The nests should be padded with material such as shredded cane fiber, shavings, or straw. This will prevent considerable egg breakage and will keep the eggs cleaner.

In transferring pullets to the laying house, do not handle them roughly. They can be taken from the growing house or shelter at night and placed on the roosts in the laying house, but the more common practice is to shut them in the growing house in the evening and transfer them early the next morning.

In making the transfer, examine the pullets carefully and separate out those which are smaller than average, as well as those which are thin, pale in face and shank, or show other evidences of lacking in health or of being inferior to the remainder of the flock. If the pullets have been properly grown, there should be few of these culls. In some flocks there may be a high proportion with crooked breastbones. While this is an undesirable condition, it does not seem to interfere particularly with egg production, and such pullets may be kept if they are satisfactory otherwise.

Many poultry raisers make a practice of giving the pullets a worm treatment when they are transferred to the laying house, and also of treating them for lice by one of the methods outlined in Chapter 6. Anti-picking devices, to prevent cannibalism, can be attached now if the pullets were not debeaked earlier, as they should have been.

Because all of this handling may cause some shock to the pullets, it is best to house them before most of them are laying. If they cannot be put in the laying house until most of them have started laying, it probably would be best to avoid any extra handling and make the transfer as easily and quickly as possible. Otherwise, they may stop laying for a few weeks and go through a light molt.

As a rule, it is best to continue the use of the growing mash until the pullets are at least 6 months of age or are laying at a rate of around 20 percent. This avoids forcing them into production too rapidly and enables them to make their full growth.

Percentage production means the number of eggs laid each day, divided by the number of pullets in the flock. For example, if 50 pullets lay 10 eggs in a day, that is 20 percent production. More than 10 hens in the flock will be laying in this instance, but not many of them will lay every day, especially in the beginning.

The percentage production should increase at a fairly rapid rate, reaching 50 to 60 percent in a matter of a month or so, especially in a small flock. The rate of production should continue to increase steadily, peaking at around 80 to 90 percent (40 to 45 eggs from a flock of 50 hens) and on occasional days every hen in the flock may lay. Occasionally, too, a hen will lay two eggs in one day.

FEEDING

There are three main systems of feeding a laying flock, although practically every poultryman has developed a few little variations of his own. While individual poultrymen may have strong preferences for one system or another, records on carefully conducted tests show there is not a great deal of difference in the results secured from the various methods, and it is largely a matter of personal preference and convenience as to which is followed.

For a small flock, especially in town, the all-mash method has much to commend it. In this system, all of the feed ingredients except grit and the lime source (oyster shell, ground limestone, etc.) are included in the ground mash mixture, and it is not necessary to feed anything else. It is a great convenience to have to keep on hand and provide containers for only one feed, especially when it must be bought in small quantities and storage space is scarce. Practically all feed companies mix an all-mash ration, or up-to-date formulas for home-mixing or custom-mixing at an elevator or mill can be secured from agricultural colleges, poultry magazines, and other sources.

In any method of feeding, it is best to put out only enough mash at one time to last the birds for about one day. This insures that they clean the old mash out of the hopper and that it does not collect in the bottom and get stale. Then, too, the addition of fresh feed each day gives the birds a new interest in it, and they will eat more of it. A good schedule would be to put mash in the hopper late in the afternoon each day. In the morning, at noon, and any other time you may be in the house, it will be helpful to run your hand or a stick along the side of the mash hopper, stirring up the old mash. This, too, gives the hens a new interest in eating it.

A second method of feeding, which is quite convenient for small flockowners and especially so for those living on farms where they may have their own whole grains, is that of keeping a mash mixture and grain in separate hoppers before the birds all of the time. While an ordinary laying mash containing around 18 percent protein may be used in this method, a more frequent recommendation is to use a special mash containing around 26 percent protein. The mash-feeding is done just as in the all-mash system, but, in addition, grains, including corn and oats, are kept in a separate hopper all of the time. If available, wheat may be mixed with the corn in almost any proportion up to equal parts, but the oats should be fed in a separate compartment. The corn may be fed either whole or cracked. The whole corn is more economical and just as satisfactory, but if the pullets have been accustomed to cracked corn on range, it may take them some time to learn to eat the whole corn. For that reason, if you expect to feed whole corn, make the change on range before the pullets begin laying. This also is true of practically all grains. Chickens are largely creatures of habit in their eating and do not take readily to radically new feeds. So use on the range the same grains you expect to use in the laying house.

The proportions of grain and mash eaten in this system will depend upon the rate of production and the protein content of the mash. For example, with a mash containing 18 to 20 percent protein, the birds probably will average only a little more grain than mash. With a 26 percent protein mash, they may consume almost two-thirds grain, and if a mash higher in protein content is used, the proportion of grain will be still greater.

With this system, commonly known as the cafeteria system, there must be plenty of feeder space—about four feet for each ten birds.

Ordinarily, hens will not get too fat on this cafeteria system of feeding if they are bred for high egg production. Inherently poor layers may get too fat, but they probably would not lay well on any ration. I have used this method with satisfaction for both White Leghorns and White Plymouth Rocks, but in all fairness I must say that this system is no longer in wide use among good poultrymen.

The third system involves hopper-feeding mash, as in the two preceding methods, and hand-feeding grain. This system is more commonly used by specialized poultrymen who give close and regular attention to their flocks and who might be classed as expert feeders. This system does give somewhat greater control over the feed consumption of the flock, and, in the hands of an experienced feeder, somewhat higher production probably can be secured. It should not be followed, however, unless the birds can be fed with strict regularity. For the small-flock owner who can't always be so regular in his attendance, one of the two preceding systems is likely to give better results.

With this mash and grain system, the grain may be almost any combination of corn, wheat, and oats, with a general recommendation that yellow corn make up half of the mixture and that oats do not form more than 25 percent of it. Barley and the sorghum grains can be used to replace the corn when they are more readily available, but as suggested before, they should be started before the pullets begin laying. Some poultrymen prefer to feed the oats separately in hoppers, putting out each morning about as much as the birds will clean up by noon or a little later.

The grain mixture may be fed all in the late afternoon an hour or two before the birds go to roost, or it may be fed about one-third in the morning and two-thirds in the late afternoon. If the litter is kept dry and fairly clean, the grain can be fed right in the litter, but most poultry raisers now prefer to feed it in hoppers, scattering it along on top of the mash and also using some supplementary hoppers to provide enough space for all of the hens to eat at one time. Feed all of the grain that the birds will eat before they go to roost. If no grain is fed in the morning, it will be all right if a little is left each night, but this should be only what they can eat within a few minutes in the morning.

Probably the most important thing in feeding is to use a good feed. A small-flock owner probably is better off to use one of the better known brands of commercial feed rather than to attempt to mix his own. The larger feed mixers not only follow the research at the agricultural colleges and experiment stations very closely, but also do a great deal of experimenting and testing for themselves. It's not always easy for a small-flock owner to get all of the necessary ingredients or to be sure of their quality. If you do want a feed formula, however, write to the poultry department at your agricultural college (see page 125 for list) for an up-to-date formula. A principal reason for not including feed formulas in this book is the fact that a formula may be outdated in a few months by new discoveries or changes in feed supplies, while your state college always is in a position to provide an up-to-date formula without cost.

The best measuring stick of feed value is profit over feed cost. Price is not always a safe criterion of feed value. Certainly never buy a feed simply because it is cheap in price—it may be of cheap quality, too. Good feed is important not only because the chickens must depend upon it for all the nutritive factors necessary for growth, health, and egg production, but the vitamin and mineral content and other nutritive properties of eggs are influenced by the diet of the hens.

SUPPLEMENTARY FEEDS

Feed consumption will vary with factors such as rate of egg production, environmental temperature, and the type of feed. Some guidelines can be given, but the important thing is to keep close watch on your own flock. A decline in feed and water consumption is usually the first sign that something is wrong. A second sign, related to the first, is a change in color or consistency of the droppings. Such changes are signals that the birds are ill or off base in some way and that a drop in egg production may show up very soon. It is important, therefore, to observe your birds until you know what is normal for them.

Changes in feed and water intake can be detected by weighing the amount given every day. A rough guide can be obtained by using a fixed measure to put out the same amount each day, increasing as the chickens consume more.

After your pullets are housed, you may expect them to continue gaining in egg production rather rapidly. Once they have reached their peak, they should maintain that approximate level of production for a few weeks, then decline very gradually until they have been laying for 12 to 15 months. This is the normal pattern and any marked variation should be cause for questioning.

If feed consumption drops or egg production begins to decline more than normal, hens sometimes can be stimulated to eat more by using some supplementary feeding. An old favorite is a moist mash, made by moistening some of the regular laying mash with milk or water until it is just crumbly. Spread it along on top of the regular feed. Shortly after noon seems to be a good time. Feed about 3 pounds per 100 birds or just what they will clean up in 15 or 20 minutes.

Pellets and crumbles, fed in the same way, have largely replaced the use of moist mash. Don't overfeed on supplements; don't begin them unless you can continue feeding them at the same time every day as long as they are needed.

Good poultrymen who want to use these supplementary feedings usually do not begin their use as long as the pullets are gaining satisfactorily in egg production in the fall. When they get up to 50 or 60 percent production, however, they are watched very closely and if they show signs of hesitation in production, such as a period of a week when production does not reach a previous high point, a light feeding of one of the supplementary feeds is begun. Usually the full quantity is not started at once, for the birds may need to learn to eat this new feed. The quantity can be gradually increased as appears necessary up to the limits suggested above. But supplementary feeding of any kind is not necessary as long as the birds lay well without it.

Checking the body weight of laying hens is another method of determining when feed consumption needs to be stimulated, for upon body weight depends much of a hen's capacity to lay eggs in winter. Loss of weight during late fall and winter usually is the forerunner of partial molting and, consequently, lowered production. Apparently the reason for this is that colder weather often results in a diversion of feed nutrients from egg manufacturing to maintaining body temperature.

If a representative group of birds in the flock is marked and weighed regularly every week or so, any average decline in body weight will be detected. Ordinarily, pullets should continue to gain in body weight during most of their first year of production. If it doesn't seem desirable to go to the trouble of weighing the birds, the same thing can be determined fairly well by handling a number of them selected at random. The presence of some surplus fat in the abdomen and a well-rounded breast indicates proper fleshing.

When weight appears to decline, it is time to introduce some weight-promoting practice, such as supplementary feeds.

The tendency of pullets to go through a partial molt in the fall or winter, more properly termed a winter pause, is largely inherited, however; so, while the stimulating practices outlined may help to modify the severity and extent of the molt, the real solution is to get stock of better breeding. But even so, the maintenance of body weight is an important factor in good management.

LIGHTING

Another method of increasing winter egg production is by the use of lights in the laying house. In fact, lights should be started before the use of supplementary feeds because lights can be arranged to require less regular attention from the poultryman. The use of lights usually will not result in any increase in the number of eggs laid during the year, but extra light will increase the proportion laid in the short days of winter.

With a small flock kept primarily to provide eggs for home consumption, it is rather doubtful whether the use of lights is justified. Most poultrymen producing eggs primarily for market use them, of course, to help get more eggs during the fall and winter when the price is highest.

There are two common methods of using lights—(1) all night and (2) sufficient to provide about a thirteen-hour day.

Automatic time switches can be purchased or made from an alarm clock to turn the lights on and off at regular hours. Regularity in the use of lights is extremely important. If such a device is available, then the use of lights in the morning to provide about thirteen hours of light for the chickens (including the natural daylight, of course) is very satisfactory. If necessary, the lights also can be used for a short time in the afternoon to finish up the feeding and caring for the chickens.

With this thirteen-hour day method, two 40-watt bulbs with reflectors will provide sufficient light for a 20-by-20-foot pen. They should hang about 6 feet above the floor in such position that the rays of light will cover the entire pen, with the heaviest concentration over the feeders and water fountains.

When no time switch is available, a simple method is to use smaller bulbs, probably about 15-watt, in a 20-by-20-foot pen, which can be turned on at bedtime and allowed to burn all night. With all night light, the heaviest concentration of light should be over the roosts.

While the benefit of the light appears primarily to be due to its effect upon the laying organs through its action upon the pituitary gland, nevertheless, it is advisable to have feed and water available all of the time. Some birds will be eating and drinking at almost any hour the lights are on.

Most breeders will have specific recommendations for lighting their birds under the various conditions under which they may be reared or housed for laying. The recommendations may vary somewhat from those which have just been outlined—and they may vary from each other—but they generally agree on at least two principles: never increase light (the length of day as determined by the combination of natural and artificial light) on growing birds; never decrease light on laying birds. They will be glad to provide details of their lighting (and other management recommendations) on request.

The relationship between the number of eggs laid and feed consumption (which is the heart of this section) has been well brought out by some studies at the Maryland Agricultural Experiment Station. It was observed that the average feed requirement for maintenance varied from 46.8 pounds for 3-pound birds to 81.4 pounds for 7-pound birds. For each 100 standard-weight eggs laid, an additional 14.2 pounds of feed were required. The pounds of feed required according to size of bird, without gain or loss in body weight, and number of eggs laid were estimated to be as follows:

3-lb. 100-egg birds,   61.0 lbs. of feed,   7.3 lbs. feed per dozen
3-lb. 200-egg birds,   75.2 "   "   "   ,   4.5 "   "   "   "
5-lb. 100-egg birds,   79.5 "   "   "   ,   9.5 "   "   "   "
5-lb. 200-egg birds,   93.7 "   "   "   ,   5.6 "   "   "   "
7-lb. 100-egg birds,   95.6 "   "   "   , 11.5 "   "   "   "
7-lb. 200-egg birds, 109.8 "   "   "   ,   6.6 "   "   "   "

Insoluble grit and a calcium supplement, such as oyster shell or limestone, should be available in small hoppers. Laying hens need to have adequate calcium for body maintenance and for making egg-shells, which are largely calcium carbonate.

Overriding all of these suggestions, however, is the strong recommendation to follow the program outlined by the manufacturer whose feed you are using or by the breeder of your pullets. This is especially important if you have a flock larger than a few dozen birds. In very small flocks there is some pleasure in trying some of the personal touches discussed above or those which follow. After all, if they aren't completely successful, you haven't suffered a great loss and you have gained some experience which will be valuable with later flocks.

The use of tender, green feed, as suggested for growing pullets, is helpful in reducing the quantity of other feeds required by hens and can be provided in the same ways as for pullets.

The use of large quantities of green feed results in increasing the yellow color of the egg yolk, however. Some consumers object to these yellow yolks; therefore, it is desirable to control the green feeding. If it is cut and fed separately, the maximum probably ought to be around 3 to 5 pounds per 100 birds daily. If the hens run in an outside pen, the green feed consumption can be controlled by keeping them confined in the house until late afternoon.

Table scraps can provide considerable feed for chickens, but should not be depended upon too heavily, for they will not provide the balance of proteins, carbohydrates, fats, minerals, and vitamins which chickens require for health and high production. It will be better if the table scraps are run through a food chopper before feeding them, and they must be fed fresh. Spoiled foods, particularly meat, or spoiled canned foods, may kill the chickens. Most vegetable parings, particularly potato peels, are not palatable unless cooked.

Table scraps should not contain the peels of citrus fruits, coffee grounds, onions, or foods or liquids containing a high concentration of salt.

If such vegetables as cabbage and mangel beets are stored for winter use, the chickens will relish them, although they should not be fed in large quantities or they may interfere with the consumption of the regular egg mash.

It is possible, too, to dry lawn clippings in a box or pan in a room where the temperature is around 70 to 80 degrees Fahrenheit. They should be stirred frequently to insure complete drying. If dried outside, they should be kept in the shade during the drying and for storage. These can be fed during the winter, after soaking, either in a wet mash or as soaked clippings. Alfalfa or clover leaves can be used in the same way. Bright green alfalfa hay can be fed in a wire rack with benefit as a source of green feed during the winter. Most mashes contain a liberal percentage of alfalfa meal, however, so an excessive amount of additional green feed should not be provided.

WATER

A constant supply of water is even more important than feed, especially in warm weather. A flock of 100 hens will actually drink around five gallons of water daily, but if a single fountain is used in the pen, it should provide for at least seven or eight gallons per 100 hens; so filling will not be required more than once a day.

There are many types of watering fountains, but the main requirements of a fountain for poultry of any age are that the water always be available and that the chickens cannot get into it with their feet. For a small flock, an open pan with a wire guard, or a large fountain with a float valve to control the flow of water, probably will be best. From the standpoint of convenience, a fountain which can be filled from the top is to be preferred if a float valve cannot be used.

When possible, water piped under pressure directly to the laying house is considered to be about the greatest labor-saver on a poultry farm. A reliable float valve on the end of the water line assures a constant supply of water. A long trough, similar to an eaves trough, covered with a wire guard frequently is used. It is well to have an overflow pipe, with the outlet of the overflow a half inch or so below the top edge of the trough or fountain. This avoids danger of soaking the litter in case the float valve should become stuck and fail to close when the fountain becomes full.

Water is just as important in winter as in summer, but the problem then is to keep it from freezing. Some poultrymen provide enough heat to keep the whole house above freezing temperature. A simpler way is to use one of the automatic electric water warmers which can be plugged into any light circuit. These contain a thermostat which turns the heater on automatically when the water temperature drops below 50 degrees. They are well worth the small cost.

If electricity is not available, lamp-heated waterers may be used, or else the fountains should be refilled often enough with warm water to provide a constant supply.

LITTER MANAGEMENT

Litter must be used on the floor of the laying house, the same as in the brooder house, and the same materials are satisfactory. A good many poultry raisers clean out the litter every week or two. This may be necessary when only a thin layer of a relatively nonabsorbent litter is used, but such a system of management results in a high litter cost, excessive time spent in cleaning, and such litter is not as satisfactory for fertilizer as that which has been used for a longer time.

Most of the more absorbent materials, such as peat moss, sugarcane fiber, and soft-wood shavings, can be used for a month to six weeks before being changed, particularly if they are stirred frequently.

A system which has attained favor is to use what is known as a "built-up" litter. This is developed by spreading two or three inches of a good litter material over the floor in late summer. It seems helpful to use an inch or so of sand over the floor under the litter, but this is not essential. This litter is kept stirred frequently and spread evenly over the floor. As it becomes pulverized, small quantities of fresh litter are added. By the time cold weather arrives, there should be a thickness of six inches of fine litter over the floor. During the winter, then, it is kept stirred but is not changed unless it becomes really wet around a fountain or where rain blows in at a window. Although this may seem like an insanitary method of litter management, there actually seems to be less development of disease germs in a deep, finely pulverized litter than in a thin layer of litter. This built-up litter can be cleaned out in the spring or used until the house is cleaned for the next group of pullets.

Built-up litter cannot be started late in the fall, and if, for some reason, it must be cleaned out in the middle of the winter, it cannot be built up again, but it will be necessary to continue it for the rest of the year with a thinner layer and more frequent changing.

Each time the house is cleaned it ought to be scraped and swept thoroughly, then sprayed with a good disinfectant which may be obtained in suitable quantities from a hatcheryman, dealer, or drugstore.

DROPPING BOARDS AND PITS

In houses where the roosts are over dropping boards, the manure should be cleaned off at least twice a week.

If dropping pits are used, they will not need to be cleaned so frequently. If the entire house is cleaned as often as once every six weeks, the pits can be cleaned out at the same time, and the droppings from the pits mixed right with the litter from the floor. If built-up litter is used, however, and cleaned only once or twice a year, then the dropping pits should be cleaned out about once every month or six weeks. If a thin layer of the litter material is spread over the floor under the dropping pits after each cleaning, it will help to keep the droppings drier and make cleaning easier.

Another helpful practice is to scatter a few pounds of superphosphate over the droppings from each dozen hens about once a week.

This can be obtained from any store handling feeds, seeds, and fertilizers. The phosphate not only tends to dry up the droppings and prevent odors, but it adds to the fertilizing value of the droppings. If phosphate is used regularly, the pits may not need to be cleaned more than once every two or three months, provided they do not become too full.

MANURE DISPOSAL

Poultry manure is a very valuable fertilizer, high in nitrogen. When mixed with the superphosphate, it is excellent for gardens, but the pure manure should never be applied directly to lawns or garden plants, as it may burn them.

If the manure is improperly handled, it loses its fertilizing value rapidly through decomposition and the formation of ammonia. For this reason, in addition to using the superphosphate, which retards the loss of ammonia, it is best to spread the manure immediately upon its removal from the poultry house. When this is impossible, it can be stored in a compost pile or in covered boxes, barrels, or a concrete pit. When stored in a compost pile, it should be completely covered with lawn clippings, leaves, weeds, or other garden refuse, and then topped with a thin layer of soil. When disposed of in this manner or kept in covered containers, flies cannot come in contact with the droppings, and objectionable odors will be avoided.

While superphosphate is most effective in conserving the nitrogen, hydrated lime is more effective as a deodorizer and in repelling flies, rats and mice. Hydrated lime also reduces nitrogen losses and improves the handling quality of the product. From 100 to 200 pounds per ton is recommended (100 if well-mixed and 200 if simply scattered over the droppings daily).

Since approximately two-thirds of the droppings are voided in the litter and one-third on the dropping board or pit, roughly one pound of superphosphate or hydrated lime scattered daily over the dropping board or pit for each 100 hens should be sufficient.

Never spread poultry litter or droppings where you expect to raise chickens within the next couple of years because of the danger of spreading disease.

A suggested application of poultry manure on gardens would be 200 to 250 pounds of the manure and litter per 1,000 square feet, plus 30 pounds of a complete garden fertilizer. The manure can be broadcast on the soil before plowing and the fertilizer broadcast and raked into the soil just before planting. Poultry manure is regarded as being twice as valuable as horse or cow manure. Poultry raisers who have more available than needed for their own ground frequently will find considerable demand for it from neighbors, to whom it may be given or sold.

BROODINESS

Even in strains bred for high production, an occasional hen will "go broody," which means that she wants to stay on the nest and incubate eggs. When a hen goes broody, she usually will be found on the nest late in the afternoon, and when she is approached she will ruffle up her feathers and object to your approaching her, even to the extent of taking a violent peck at your hand. If allowed to have her own way, a broody hen is likely to stay on the nest for several weeks, laying no eggs in the meantime.

If the very first night she is noticed, however, she is taken to a coop with a wire or slatted bottom, her broodiness can be cured within two or three days and she may be laying again within a few weeks. The broody coop can be built of wire and fastened to one wall of the laying house or over the roosts in a large house. It needs to be only large enough to hold two or three hens in a flock of 100 hens. Feed and water should be provided generously to broody hens, either in small troughs or cans fastened to the coop. Return the hen to the flock as soon as she gets over her broodiness. If she should not be completely cured, however, and should start in again, repeat the treatment.

HOW LONG TO KEEP HENS

Pullets hatched in the spring usually will begin laying in the fall about six months later and will lay for approximately a year, some more and some less.

They then stop laying for a period of time ranging from a mere "slow down" to a complete stoppage of laying for three or four months. During this time they lose their old feathers and grow new ones. This is known as molting.

During their second year of production, hens will average about 30 percent fewer eggs than during the first year, depending somewhat upon their breeding and production during the first year. These yearling hens will very likely be carriers of diseases to which they may have developed immunity. When they are retained and housed with the next flock of pullets, the pullets are almost certain to suffer ill effects from the mixture, even if they are separated by partitions. Selling all of the old flock each year and housing only new pullets will provide more eggs and simplify management. For these reasons smallflock owners probably would be better off to dispose of all their hens in the fall and replace them with a new flock of pullets.

CULLING

During the year an occasional hen will stop laying for one cause or another. If she is recognized right away, she can be used for food or sold, and the feed she would have eaten will be saved. Also, if one wishes to keep over a part of the hens for a second year, it is desirable to be able to select the best ones to keep. This selection of nonlayers at any time is generally known as culling.

In yellow-skinned breeds, which includes practically all of those commonly kept, the yellow color fades from the various parts of the body as laying progresses, and returns when laying has stopped. Therefore, at any time it is possible to tell something about the production of a hen by examining this pigmentation. The following table shows the approximate time it takes to lose the pigment from the various parts of the body when a hen is laying at a fair rate of production and the approximate time it takes for the pigment to return to those same parts of the body when she stops laying.

Part of Hen	Approximate Laying Time To Lose Color	Approximate Vacation Time To Gain Color
Vent	0–3 days	0–1 days
Eye ring	5–7 days	3–5 days
Beak and earlobes**	4–6 weeks	10–14 days
Shanks	5–7 months	4–8 weeks

**Applies to breeds with white earlobes.

In addition, a laying hen will have a soft, full, red comb, bright, alert eyes, and generally healthy, active appearance. A hen which is not laying will have a dried, shriveled comb, pale in color, and she usually will not be as alert and active as a good layer.

The abdomen of a good layer usually is rather large, soft and pliable, while the nonlayer has an abdomen that is full of hard fat. The pubic bones (one of which can be felt on each side of the vent) will be at least three fingers' width apart in a good layer, while they will be unyielding and close together in a nonlayer.

In the fall of the year at the molting season, the molt also helps to distinguish between the good and poor layers. Hens which stop laying and begin molting by the middle of August or earlier usually are the poorest layers in the flock, while the later into the fall a hen lays before she molts, the better she is.

The following table summarizes the various points to be considered in selecting nonlayers:

CHARACTERISTICS IDENTIFYING LAYERS AND NONLAYERS

	Condition in a—	
Character	*Layer*	*Nonlayer*
Comb	Large, bright red, smooth, glossy	Dull, dry, shriveled, scaly
Face	Bright red	Yellow tint
Vent	Enlarged, smooth, moist	Shrunken, puckered, dry
Pubic bones	Thin, pliable, spread apart	Blunt, rigid, close together
Abdomen	Expanded, soft, pliable	Contracted, hard, fleshy
Lateral processes	Prominent, pliable	Hard to find, stiff
Skin	Soft, loose	Thick, underlaid with fat

CHARACTERISTICS INDICATING WHETHER PREVIOUS PRODUCTION WAS CONTINUOUS OR BRIEF

	Condition associated with—	
Character	*Continuous Laying*	*Brief Laying*
Vent	Bluish white	Yellow tint or flesh color
Eye ring and earlobe	White	Tinted with yellow
Beak	White	Tinted with yellow
Shanks	White, rather flattened	Yellow, round
Plumage	Worn, soiled	Not much worn
Molting	Late, rapid	Early, slow

CHARACTERISTICS OF A HIGH-LAYING STRAIN

Time of maturity	Laying begins at about 5 months of age in the case of Leghorns and at about 6 months in the case of Rhode Island Reds, Plymouth Rocks, and similar breeds.
Rate of production	Average of 200 or more eggs a year.
Broodiness	Birds are seldom broody.
Persistence of production	Hens are laying well in August and September toward the end of the first laying year or after it is completed.

Nonlayers should be removed any time they are seen. In larger flocks, the birds should be handled and the nonlayers culled out at least every two or three months and every month during July, August and September.

PRODUCTION STANDARD

How many eggs should a hen lay? As can be imagined, there are tremendous differences in egg production of individual hens due to variations in breeding and management. The following table shows the production goals one breeder suggests by 4-week periods beginning at 22 weeks of age:

AN EGG-PRODUCTION GOAL FOR PULLETS

4-Week Period	No. of Eggs (Hen-housed)	Percentage Production (Hen-day) In Fourth Week of Each Period
1	6.5	47.0
2	22.3	90.3
3	24.8	90.0
4	24.1	87.7
5	23.3	85.0
6	22.2	82.4
7	21.5	79.7
8	20.5	77.0
9	19.8	74.4
10	18.9	71.7
11	18.1	69.0
12	17.2	66.4
13	16.5	63.7
Total	255.7	

These are high goals, but not exceptional, and enough flocks do this well to make it worth striving for. Many individual hens exceed 300 eggs in a year. The highest known official egg record was set by a hen in an Australian egg laying contest; she reached a total of 364 eggs in 365 days.

FLYING

To keep hens from flying out of their pen, clip the large primary feathers of one wing only. This unbalances the bird when she attempts to fly and makes it impossible for her to rise high enough to get over a fence. If they have plenty of feed and water, however, hens will seldom fly over a fence five or more feet high even when no wing is clipped.

LAYING CAGES

The use of laying cages has become the most common method of housing hens in large flocks. A standard size of cage is 12 by 18 inches, holding three hens, but you also will find single-bird cages and those holding more than three.

Arrangement of the cages varies from level double rows of single-hen cages back to back to multiple decks, usually in stair-step fashion, according to the ideas of the manufacturer or the poultrymen who use them.

They are used in houses ranging from a completely open shelter in warm climates to controlled environment houses in colder areas. The latter houses are windowless, well-insulated, and with controlled temperature. Hens in a single building may number in the tens of thousands.

Poultrymen have adopted cages because of the environment control possible, the opportunity to observe the condition of individual birds, better control of some health and parasite problems, and the lower labor requirement.

Cages include an automatic watering system; feeding is automatic or by use of handy carts; both lighting and ventilation are controlled automatically. Eggs roll to the front of the cage—often onto a belt which carries them directly to the egg-packing room.

While floor management may be preferable for small flocks, if you can get a section of cages from a nearby poultryman, they can be used in almost any room or building which is well-insulated and well-ventilated without drafts. The ceiling should be eight to ten feet high, and it should be possible to keep the room temperature above 40 degrees Fahrenheit.

EGG RECORD

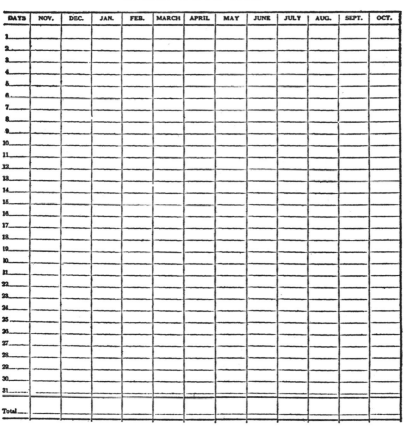

DAYS	NOV.	DEC.	JAN.	FEB.	MARCH	APRIL	MAY	JUNE	JULY	AUG.	SEPT.	OCT.
1												
2												
3												
4												
5												
6												
7												
8												
9												
10												
11												
12												
13												
14												
15												
16												
17												
18												
19												
20												
21												
22												
23												
24												
25												
26												
27												
28												
29												
30												
31												
Total												

A simple form on which a record of daily egg production can be kept for an entire year. One of these record sheets should be tacked up in each pen and a pencil hung by it for convenience.

6

Controlling Diseases and Parasites

Like other animals, chickens are subject to numerous diseases and parasites against which poultry raisers must exercise eternal vigilance or heavy losses may be suffered. In fact, disease is the chief hindrance to success in raising poultry.

Fear of diseases and parasites should not hinder anyone from endeavoring to raise poultry, for means of control have been worked out for most of the common diseases and parasites which are likely to be encountered, but a poultry raiser, large or small, would be foolish indeed to ignore the existence of these diseases and to fail to take the recommended steps to avoid loss from them.

PREVENTION

Most of the common diseases and parasites of chickens can be avoided through sound methods of management, feeding, sanitation, and preventive treatment.

Management and sanitation are closely allied, for sanitation, with poultry, does not mean hospital cleanliness. It means rather, avoidance of those conditions and circumstances which promote the reproduction and growth of disease organisms and parasites and their transmission to healthy birds. Among the factors of management and sanitation which are extremely important in preventing loss from disease and parasites are the following:

1. The thorough cleaning, scrubbing, and disinfecting of the poultry houses, both brooder and laying houses, between the disposal of one group of birds and the entrance of another. To bring new birds into a dirty house is simply asking for trouble.

To clean, remove the portable equipment from the house, then take out all loose droppings and litter material. Brush down ceilings and walls. Scrape the floors and sweep them clean. Scrub ceilings, walls, and floor with a detergent in water—hot water is preferable. If you have a high-pressure sprayer available, it is an excellent cleaning tool.

Thorough cleaning removes most of the contamination and disinfection should complete the job. No disinfectant will do its best in dirt and filth; so the more thorough the cleaning, the more effective the disinfection will be.

As soon as the final washdown of the house is completed, spray disinfectant on the ceilings, walls, and floor. Make it reach into every crack and crevice. Treat all of the fixed equipment as you do the house. Clean and disinfect all portable equipment before you return it to the house.

There are several different types and numerous brands of disinfectants available. Your poultry-supply dealer can help you choose one for your purpose. Read the label carefully to determine its suitability and for any restrictions on its use.

All disinfectants are poisonous to some degree. Handle them with care and store them in a safe place, away from children and animals.

Do not spill insecticide on your skin or clothing. If you do spill some, wash thoroughly. Don't clean spray equipment or dump excess spray material near ponds, streams, or wells.

2. Never allow chickens, either young stock or old, to run on ground used by previous flocks of chickens, young or old, in the previous two years. Neither should ground be used which has had poultry-house litter and droppings scattered on it within that period. Many poultry raisers violate this rule, sometimes without any bad results for many years, due to the fact that no diseases or parasites have become established in their flock. Sooner or later, however, trouble is certain to follow violation of this management rule, for many of the most destructive diseases and parasites live for relatively long periods of time in the soil. The range should be well-drained and so located that the drainage from the previous year's range or from another poultry flock does not run onto it.

3. Keep baby chicks and growing birds entirely separated from

the adult flock. Under no circumstances should they be allowed to run together in the same house or in the same pen, and the more complete the separation, the better. Many of the most successful poultrymen go so far as to permit no transfer of equipment, feed sacks, or utensils from the premises of the old birds to those of the young, and even have a separate caretaker for the young stock. Sometimes even a separate farm is used for rearing them.

4. Do not bring stock, particularly adult birds, from some other flock and mix them immediately with your own flock. Hold them in a separate building for three or four weeks to make sure they are carrying no communicable diseases. An even better plan is to house the new birds with a few culls from your own flock for the few weeks quarantine period to see whether any diseases are spread to them.

5. It may seem inhospitable, but trouble will be avoided many times if you do not permit visitors to enter your houses or pens. Diseases and parasites can be carried from one flock to another on shoes. In this same connection, some poultry raisers who must take care of both the old birds and baby chicks keep a pair of rubber overshoes at the brooder house which they put on whenever entering the brooder house or pen or when taking care of the young stock on range. Instead of separate overshoes, a coco mat saturated with stock dip (renewed frequently) may be kept at the entrance to the brooder house or range and all visitors, including yourself, be required to wipe their shoes carefully on it.

6. Sparrows, pigeons, and other birds may carry diseases and parasites which affect chickens. Use one-inch mesh wire screen or netting to keep them out of the chicken houses. Rats also may carry diseases and this provides one additional reason for making houses ratproof and for making sure that there are no harboring places for them.

7. Use a good feed. For health and productivity, chickens require a very complete ration, including not only the usual proteins, carbohydrates, and fats in proper proportions, but they also require minerals and most of the known vitamins. One list includes 33 nutrient requirements. Baby chicks and older chickens raised in confinement must depend upon the feed for all their nutritive needs, and a low grade of feed will have its effect in lowered health or production. Even though a low-grade feed should not result in any direct nutritive disorder, it may so weaken the health or lower the resistance of the birds that they will be more susceptible to contagious diseases and parasites.

There are numerous well-recognized conditions which develop as the result of deficiencies in the diet, usually deficiencies in vitamins, minerals, or trace elements. Among these are leg weakness in chicks, and problems with thin-shelled eggs—although the thin shells can also result from disease. The specific deficiencies to suspect first in these conditions is vitamin D and/or calcium.

Sometimes another leg trouble occurs in broilers. The legs become bowed and the hock (knee) joints are enlarged because the tendons slip over the hock joints. The condition is commonly known as slipped tendons or, more technically, perosis. It apparently results from a deficiency of manganese in the diet, although other elements may be involved.

Dietary troubles will rarely be encountered if a good, up-to-date ration is being fed according to directions.

8. Know about vaccinations. Chicks or pullets probably will have been vaccinated for some diseases when you get them. There are four major respiratory diseases for which there are effective vaccines: Newcastle disease, bronchitis, fowl pox and laryngotracheitis. Vaccinations for all these diseases will not be necessary in all areas. Where they are needed, however, they are administered at different ages. When you get your chicks or pullets, ask your supplier which vaccinations have been given and his recommendations for any additional ones at a later date. If you want to administer any of them yourself, be sure to inquire about the regulations in your state. Then follow exactly instructions for care and administration of the vaccine.

9. Provide comfortable houses with plenty of room. They should be well-ventilated, but free from drafts.

10. Always burn or bury deeply all dead birds and offal. A rather simple method of disposing of dead birds and offal is to dig a rather large hole (the exact size will vary with the size of the flock, but on one farm of 5,000 hens, a hole 4 feet in diameter and about 12 feet deep had hardly started to fill after several years' use). Old lumber, bricks, or concrete blocks may be used to shape up the sides so that the hole will not fill prematurely.

Cover it with two layers of two-inch planks, the top layer at right angles to the first, for the unit will last a long time and the planks should not rot away. In the center of the plank a round hole nine inches in diameter is cut. A piece of nine-inch galvanized sheet-iron pipe with strips cut at one end which can be bent out and nailed to the plank is fastened so that the pipe is over the center hole in the plank. The pipe extends up about 30 inches (or any other convenient height) and has a fly-tight cover. The planks then are covered with a few inches of soil. To dispose of dead birds, simply drop them down the pipe. No lime or other decaying aid is needed, although a small amount dropped over the birds periodically will hasten their decay.

11.   Remove all obviously sick chickens from the flock. It usually is best to kill them and dispose of the carcasses by burning or burying. If birds are to be treated, put them in a separate pen or hospital coop as far away from the other birds as convenient.

12.   If you have a disease outbreak in your flock, get an accurate diagnosis as soon as possible from your veterinarian or your nearest poultry diagnostic laboratory.

PARASITES

The principal parasites of poultry are lice, mites, ticks, and worms.

The body louse is the one most commonly found on chickens. If the soft feathers around the vent, thighs, or breast are parted, the tiny amber-colored parasites can be seen on the feathers, usually running to hide themselves. There also are several other types of lice. They all live on the birds and annoy by biting or chewing. Eventually, they can affect growth and egg production of the chickens. You also may find the nits (eggs) clinging to the feathers. Examine a few birds for lice every couple of weeks.

Theoretically, if louse-free pullets are placed in a house from which all old hens have been removed and which has been thoroughly cleaned and disinfected, the pullets never should become infested with lice or mites. They can be introduced, however, by sparrows and other birds.

There are several types of mites, some of which live on the birds and affect them by causing severe irritation or feather loss. The most common mite, however, the red mite, does not stay on the chickens. You may never see it on the birds because it feeds only at night when the hens are on the roosts or nests. During the day, it hides in cracks and crevices around the roosts and nests. Examine these areas carefully for whitish fuzz-like material or small "salt-and-pepper" deposits. If you find such deposits, mites likely are present and you may find them if you dig into the hiding places. Watch for them on range shelters also—in fact, wherever chickens roost. I have seen summer quarters of pullets so badly infested with mites that the pullets refused to roost in the buildings.

When lice or mites are found, treat the birds (and buildings in the case of red mites) with a federally approved insecticide, using it according to the manufacturer's directions. New products may be introduced and approval of old ones withdrawn at any time, so take care in your selection. Ask your veterinarian or county agent. You may also locate suitable products among the insecticides on the shelves of your druggist or poultry-supply dealer, as you would find garden insecticides. Sometimes, individual-bird treatment is necessary for prompt, effective control.

WORMS

There are several kinds of worms, the most common of which are large roundworms and tapeworms. The use of uncontaminated soil (that is, where no chickens have run for a few years) is extremely important in avoiding roundworms, while tapeworms are most frequently carried by flies, slugs, beetles, and similar insects.

When young stock is rather pale and unthrifty without the appearance of any specific disease, worms may be suspected. At any time when there is suspicion that the birds are infested with worms, either kill one or two for examination or carefully examine the length of the intestines of a bird killed for home use.

Special worm treatments in the form of liquid, powder, or individual capsules are available. The same drugs will not eliminate all kinds of worms; therefore, it is necessary to know definitely which type of worm is present, or else use a combination treatment. After treatment, birds can become reinfested with worms within a month or so which makes sanitation to prevent infestation the best procedure.

DISEASES

Only a few of the diseases, those most likely to be found in small flocks and most easily recognized, will be discussed. In a book of this character there does not seem to be any point in listing diseases which are not very common or which are difficult for the small-flock owner to recognize and treat.

Pullorum. This disease is transmitted from the hen through the egg to the chick, and also from infected chicks to healthy chicks. Hens carrying the disease can be detected by a test known as the pullorum test or bloodtest. Practically all hatcheries now test their breeding flocks, and chicks should not be purchased from a breeder who does not test. If no chicks or other chickens are brought onto the premises except from flocks which have been tested, little or no trouble from this disease should ever be experienced.

But if the chicks are infected, the disease will show up within the first week or two. The chicks will be droopy and will huddle together as though chilled. The disease was formerly called white diarrhea because of the customary diarrhea and pasting of the vent.

Some drugs may reduce the mortality but there really is no treatment for affected chicks other than giving them the best possible care, being especially careful to provide the recommended brooding temperature.

Baby chicks may show a diarrhea and other symptoms commonly found in pullorum disease, but which are due to improper brooding conditions, such as overheating, chilling, or a digestive disturbance. Here, too, prevention by providing proper brooding conditions is the cure.

Coccidiosis. At the present time, this is probably the most serious of all the diseases of growing chickens. It most commonly appears in chicks between one and four months of age, although it can be present in younger or older birds.

There are several different types of coccidiosis, but the one best known is the acute type, in which there are bloody droppings, and the ceca or blind guts are severely extended.

Coccidiosis is a soil- or filth-borne disease—another reason for maintaining clean houses and using uncontaminated ground. The form in which it exists for many months in the filth of poultry houses or soil on which infected birds have run is extremely resistant to destruction. For this reason, and the fact that it can be easily carried on the feet, feed sacks, or equipment, it may show up in new broods of chicks in a completely new location. It also may show up in broods where every effort has been made to maintain sanitary conditions.

Instead of attempting to keep the birds absolutely free of the disease, therefore, most poultrymen operate on the theory that a modest infection of coccidiosis produces immunity or at least a higher resistance to the disease. This is the function of most coccidiostats used in the feed. Some coccidiostats, however, are used to prevent the disease entirely or to treat flocks which show evidence of the disease.

If coccidiosis shows up, affected birds will stand huddled up, with ruffled feathers, paleness, and diarrhea. Some birds may die very soon after symptoms are noticed.

Leukosis. Lymphoid leukosis may affect pullets nearing laying age or those already laying. Cause of the disease is unknown and there is no treatment. Clean brooding entirely separate from older birds may help prevent it but does not provide a sure control. Infected birds become unthrifty, lose weight, and eventually die.

At any one time there may be only a few birds showing symptoms. In a postmortem examination, affected birds probably will have numerous internal tumors, particularly of the liver.

Marek's Disease. Once thought to be a part of the leukosis complex, it has been found that this disease is caused by a herpes virus. Control is by vaccination of the chicks—usually done at the hatchery.

Newcastle Disease. This is a highly contagious disease caused by a virus. It may affect chickens of any age. There is no effective treatment but it can be prevented by vaccination. Ask your chick supplier about vaccination; if the disease isn't present in your area, he may recommend against vaccination.

Infectious Bronchitis. This is another contagious respiratory disease, indicated by sneezing and coughing. It also can be prevented by vaccination. Ask your chick supplier about it for the vaccinations for Newcastle and bronchitis may be given in combination.

Infectious Laryngotracheitis. A third contagious respiratory disease. In addition to coughing and sneezing, the birds have difficulty in breathing. They gasp for air, usually with the head extended and held upward with mouth open. A trachea (windpipe) filled with bloody mucus is a definite indication of the disease. It is not a problem in all areas, but, in those where it does exist, vaccination will prevent it. There is no effective treatment. Destroy affected birds and keep the house warm and dry with draft-free ventilation.

Fowl Pox. This is a highly contagious disease and appears as nodules on the head, comb, wattles, and around the eyes. Sometimes the inside of the mouth and even the windpipe and lungs are affected with ulcers.

If the outbreak is noticed as soon as one or two birds have it, these should be removed and destroyed, then the house thoroughly cleaned and disinfected. It is doubtful whether individual treatment of affected birds is worthwhile.

When fowl pox is present in other flocks in the community, or if previous flocks on your farm have been infected, then the growing pullets should be vaccinated each year. The vaccine and complete instructions for vaccinating can be obtained through your hatchery-man or a local veterinarian, or, in most states, direct from vaccine manufacturers. Since the vaccine contains the live virus, however, it should be handled with caution and all young birds on the farm should be vaccinated at the same time.

Colds and Roup. Colds (properly known as infectious coryza) in chickens, as in humans, although infectious, are most likely to appear in birds which are run-down due to improper nutrition or infestation with parasites. Improper housing, resulting in drafts or excessive moisture in the house, will aggravate an outbreak of colds.

Remove affected birds—those with running noses, or those which sneeze and show difficulty in breathing—and feed them well. Some additional green feed and vitamins A and D in cod-liver oil or in other form may help. Sometimes sulfa drugs are used for treatment. Ask your veterinarian or poultry specialist about his experience in using any treatment.

The condition generally known as roup, in which the head of the bird swells around the eyes, is generally the result of a cold condition allowed to go too long without treatment. There really is little which can be done for such birds, and it would be best to destroy them.

Colds, as well as several other respiratory disorders, are harbored by recovered birds which then become carriers capable of spreading the disease to susceptible birds. When new pullets are brought in from range, therefore, and are brought in contact with these "carriers," they usually become infected with colds. This accounts for the fact that on many poultry farms colds occur every year within a few weeks after the pullets are housed.

If all of the old hens are sold each fall before the new pullets are housed, and if the laying house is thoroughly cleaned and disinfected before the birds are brought in, it should be possible to break the cycle and eliminate the disease from the farm.

Impacted Crop. Sometimes chicks eat litter, dry grass, string, or other materials which clog the outlet of the crop, the organ to which the food goes when it is swallowed. The chick may or may not continue to eat well, but the crop usually swells considerably, due either to the fact that everything eaten remains in it or to the formation of gas.

Sometimes by holding the bird head downward and massaging the crop, the contents can be worked out through the mouth. Injecting water into the crop may help in cleaning it out.

If this treatment doesn't succeed, an incision can be made through the skin and wall of the crop and the contents removed, then the opening sewed up with heavy white thread. Withhold water for about a day, then give water and moistened food for two or three days. Chickens do not appear to be particularly sensitive to pain nor do they become easily infected; so there need be little hesitation at undertaking an operation of this kind.

Bumblefoot. Sometimes the feet of chickens will show a rather severe swelling, particularly between the toes, and with a rather hard core on the bottom of the foot.

This condition is known as bumblefoot and may be caused by a bruise or injury incurred when chickens jump from high roosts, nests, or feeders, to a hard, bare floor. Infection is also probably present.

The hard core can be removed and the wound bandaged, but treatment is hardly worthwhile, and seriously affected birds should be destroyed. The less seriously affected birds may recover unaided.

Tuberculosis. Tuberculosis is most common in flocks where conditions are very insanitary and where birds are kept until they are several years of age. It does not usually seriously affect birds until their second year of production. Poultry raisers who replace all of their hens with pullets each year will practically never have tuberculosis in their flocks. It is important to avoid tuberculosis in poultry because the same form which affects chickens also affects hogs and causes severe losses.

If a flock of very valuable birds is infected, there is a diagnostic test which can be applied by a veterinarian and which will permit the detection and elimination of infected birds.

Frozen Combs. In severely cold weather, the combs and wattles may freeze, particularly on the Mediterranean breeds which have such large ones. Thaw them gradually with snow or cold water and rub the affected parts with vaseline.

Since frozen combs may make males incapable of fertilizing eggs for a week or ten days, they should be prevented by warming the house in cold weather. Cutting off the combs and wattles, known as dubbing, also is effective prevention, not only of freezing but of other types of injury. Cut them close to the head with sharp shears on a warm day. Give dubbed birds plenty of water to drink. About ten weeks of age seems to be the best time to do it, although they can be dubbed at earlier or later ages.

Cannibalism. The tendency of growing chicks and adult birds to pick at one another is not a disease, but is one of the most aggravating vices to which chickens are heir, and causes more worry and loss than many diseases.

It may show up in very small chicks with the tendency to pick at the toes, and tails, or wing joints of other chicks, and the habit persists throughout the growing period.

Cannibalism appears to be primarily a management problem, although there are some manifestations of it which are not explainable. One of the most common management mistakes which promotes the cannibalistic tendency is to overcrowd the chicks. Allow a minimum of 35 square feet per 100 chicks at the start, and more space is better. Double this space at six weeks of age.

Bright spots of sunlight which start the chicks to picking at toes or beaks may result in an outbreak of cannibalism. Many poultrymen now use cloth curtains or shades to darken the interior of the brooder house so that there will be no bright areas, and the chicks cannot see each other quite so well, in case bleeding is started through injury. Care must be taken, of course, not to shut off the ventilation.

Chicks which are kept confined to the house are more likely to develop cannibalistic habits than those running outside. Feeding green feeds to confined chicks may be of help. Keep feed and water before them all of the time, so that they will be kept busy eating and drinking.

Once an outbreak starts, the injured chicks can be treated with red, bitter-tasting salves, available at hatcheries and dealers, and which are designed not only to promote healing of the injured birds, but to discourage picking by the rest of the flock. The use of special red paint on the windows, which makes it impossible for the chicks to distinguish blood on picked birds, may be helpful in the case of confined flocks.

If no other action seems to stop the outbreak, the hard tip of the upper beak can be removed by cutting slightly into the edge of the beak about ⅛ inch back of the tip and prying and pulling the tip off.

Some hatcheries debeak chicks before delivery. They use precision electric debeakers which they sometimes will rent to poultrymen for use when the chicks are older. If the debeaking is done with a knife, it probably will have to be repeated from time to time. Even if the chicks are debeaked with an electric debeaker at hatching time, they likely will need to be debeaked again—at least "touched up"—at about 12 weeks of age. It should not be delayed longer than about 16 weeks or it may affect maturity and egg production of the pullets. If the first debeaking can be delayed until the pullets are about 12 weeks old, it probably will need to be done only once.

Losses from cannibalism can be extremely serious in a laying flock, especially just after the pullets are housed. This may start through eversion of the oviduct (known as prolapsus) when a pullet lays, or there may be slight bleeding at the time the egg is laid. Other birds get started picking at the injured part and continue until the bird is killed. Such occurrences are also known as "blowouts" or "pickouts." Proper debeaking of the young pullets provides effective prevention. If the birds were not debeaked, there are plastic or metal devices which can be attached to the beak. These make it difficult for the bird to pick straight ahead but do not hinder eating.

Egg Eating. Sometimes hens learn to break and eat eggs. This seldom will happen if the nests are somewhat darkened and if the eggs are gathered at least three times a day so that there is less likelihood of breakage. Usually only one or two hens learn the trick and can be spotted by close watching. If an egg eater is identified, trim her beak as for cannibalism or dispose of her. If you are unable to locate the offender, sometimes a "planted" egg filled with hot pepper or similarly unpalatable material will cure her.

Fly control. Flies spread some diseases and parasites. But more im-

(See chapter on CONTROLLING DISEASES AND PARASITES *for the following illustrations.)*

What happens when feed is deficient in an essential vitamin. Bird on the left received sufficient vitamin G; bird on the right, insufficient. Chicks are from the same hatch.
(Cornell Agricultural Experiment Station)

Characteristic pose of chick with rickets.
(University of Wisconsin)

Chick showing typical leg condition known as "slipped tendons" or "perosis."
(University of Wisconsin)

Swollen condition of the foot, known as "bumblefoot."

Chick showing typical symptoms of coccidiosis.

Characteristic posture of pullet with fowl paralysis.

Characteristic pose of bird with infectious laryngotracheitis. (*Dr. Salsbury's Laboratories*)

Bird with severe fowl pox infection.
(*Dr. Salsbury's Laboratories*)

Hen with infectious coryza (commonly called "roup"). Note typically dirty wing where she has been wiping her head.
(*Dr. Salsbury's Laboratories*)

Two devices to prevent cannibalism among mature chickens. The one at left prevents bird from seeing straight ahead; the one at right prevents picking except when head is lowered. Both are effective.

Excellent head of an excellent layer. She produced 308 eggs.

Head of a hen that laid 94 eggs in her first year.

In pedigree breeding, as chick is removed from incubator, a numbered wing band is attached for permanent identification.

In pedigree breeding, eggs from each hen are incubated together in a small basket or bag, so chicks will not become mixed until their parentage has been recorded.

portant is the fact that they are objectionable to people. Your family won't want them around; neither will your neighbors.

If a small flock is confined, the simplest procedure may be to make the poultry house fly-tight and/or use electrical grids or mechanical fly traps.

Also practice good housekeeping methods in the buildings and around the yards. Dispose of dead birds and offal promptly. Keep the feed room clean, as well as the egg storage room, and all space related to the poultry. Keep poultry yards neatly mowed. Dispose of garbage and all wastes by burying or holding in fly-tight containers until hauled away.

Keep manure pits screened or clean out the manure frequently in warm weather.

Finally, chemical fly sprays may be used but be sure to follow instructions carefully, especially where eggs are being held. Judge the value of a fly spray by how few flies you see still living—not by the number of dead ones you see.

PREDATORS

When pullets are grown on range, or even in yards, be aware of likely predators—hawks, owls, crows, foxes, skunks, weasels, and dogs. At night, keep the pullets in closed shelters. If bothered during the day, find out whether shooting is permissible.

An electric fence wire slightly above ground level on the outside of the range fence can discourage predators. Predators provide one reason for confinement rearing.

RATS AND MICE

Losses, including chickens, feed, and other items eaten or destroyed by rats and mice, may total many dollars a year. I'll never forget the shock of going into the brooder house one morning and finding twenty dead six-week-old chicks scattered around the floor. None was badly eaten, but each had a slight wound on the neck or head. Suspecting rats, for it was an old building with an excellent rat harbor under its wooden floor, I carefully examined the floor and walls and finally found the hole where the rodents had entered.

Rats are not easy either to trap or poison, but the best control is to have buildings as nearly ratproof as possible and to provide no piles of trash or refuse where they may hide. If poisoning is attempted, the secret of success is to use the unpoisoned food as a prebait until they are eating it readily, then feed the poisoned food in exactly the same way.

GENERAL

While the most common poultry diseases, parasites, and predators have been discussed here, there are many others which make occasional appearances. Since the symptoms of a good many diseases are rather similar and it is not particularly easy to diagnose poultry ailments, it frequently will be desirable to get help from someone more experienced. This may be a local veterinarian, hatcheryman, service man, county agent, vocational agriculture teacher, or others.

The value of individual birds is so small that it will seldom pay to go to much expense to get a diagnosis or treatment if only one or two birds are affected. If there seems to be a general outbreak in the flock, however, then it will be worthwhile to get an accurate diagnosis, and the quicker this is done, the better. Proper treatment cannot be begun until you know what is causing the trouble.

If you have access to a poultry diagnostic laboratory—either state- or privately-operated—taking some birds there for examination may be your best course of action. Your hatcheryman or county agent can tell you whether there is one within a reasonable distance.

The pathologists at such a laboratory like to see live birds typical of the problem—preferably one just beginning to show symptoms, one definitely sick, and one close to death. Deliver them as quickly as possible, handling them carefully and humanely. Be prepared to give a history of the problem, including information on any changes in feed consumption, egg production, or other behavior.

I hope this chapter won't discourage your interest in having chickens. Actually, the hazards are no greater than with any other live animals, but it seems better to alert you to potential problems than to leave you unaware that there are any.

7

Breeding for Improvement

Since it is almost impossible to do a really worthwhile job of breeding with a small flock, a chapter on this subject may seem out of place in this book. Perhaps a brief discussion will give small poultrymen a better appreciation of the extreme value and importance of good breeding, however, and may lay the groundwork for a sound program of breeding in case they might wish to undertake it later on.

If one is keeping one of the more common breeds and buys chicks from good hatcherymen or breeders, it probably will not be possible to make very much improvement in the stock unless a pedigree-breeding program is followed, which is expensive and time-consuming. When some of the less popular breeds which have been less intensively bred for egg production are kept, some progress probably can be made without trapnesting and pedigree breeding.

BREEDING FOR EGG PRODUCTION

Five separate genetic or breeding factors have been shown to be largely responsible for a bird's egg record, according to the University of Massachusetts. These five factors are: (1) early sexual maturity; (2)

freedom from winter pause; (3) high intensity or high rate of production; (4) nonbroodiness; (5) persistency.

Three of these factors can be determined without trapnesting. Early sexual maturity is indicated by the age when a pullet lays her first egg. The most desirable age at first egg varies by breed, ranging from about 160 to 200 days. Pullets which begin laying within this age-range should be marked with a colored-celluloid spiral leg band.

Pullets which go broody during the laying year should be marked with a band of a different color.

Persistency can be measured by the length of the laying year of each pullet. This should not be less than 315 days, and the longer a pullet lays, the higher she would rate for this factor. Therefore, pullets which still are laying 315 days after they begin should be marked with a leg band of a third color.

Therefore, at the end of the laying year, those pullets showing early sexual maturity, nonbroodiness, and persistency, will likely be the better birds.

Many birds with excellent egg records, however, should not be used for breeding purposes because of such serious defects as feathers on the shanks or between the toes in clean-legged breeds; side sprigs on the combs; slipped or split wings; crooked backs; crooked breastbones; foreign color in shanks, face, ear lobes, and plumage; and serious departures from standard weights.

To mate with the hens which do meet the desirable standards, be sure to use good males, for the male is at least half the flock. He not only should be a good specimen of the breed, but should show a high degree of vigor and aggressiveness.

If at all possible, the males should be bought as individually pedigreed birds, secured preferably as hatching eggs or day-old chicks to reduce the chances of bringing in communicable disease. These should be bought from outstanding breeders.

One male will be required for each 12 to 20 hens, according to the breed (fewer males in the light breeds, like Leghorns, and more males in the heavier breeds); size of flock (fewer males are needed proportionately in a large flock than in a small one); the season of the year (if mating is started early in the hatching season, it is well to start with a few extra males, then if a few are lost during the season, it will not be necessary to introduce new ones); and upon the vigor of the birds.

Mate the flock at least two weeks before hatching eggs are to be saved. Also check with your county agent or state poultry department regarding any regulations about the production of hatching eggs, particularly bloodtesting. That is a requirement in some states.

PEDIGREE BREEDING

The modern method of breeding is to select breeding birds on the basis of their family characteristics rather than the qualities of the individual birds alone. To determine family characteristics accurately, as well as to get accurate records on the two other genetic factors for high egg production (freedom from winter pause and high intensity), as well as other desirable characteristics, such as the shape, color, and weight of eggs, etc., it is necessary to trapnest each hen and keep an accurate record of the parentage of each chick and an accurate record of the performance of each chick.

Trapnesting is the use of nests with a type of closure which shuts when the hen enters the nest, preventing another hen from entering the same nest, and preventing the hen which has entered from leaving until she is released by an attendant. Each hen is marked with a numbered leg band for identification. When the attendant releases a hen from the trapnest, he notes her leg band number and makes a mark opposite her number on a ruled record sheet if she has laid an egg, after which the hen is released back into the pen.

The egg also is numbered with the leg band number of the hen which laid it. All of the eggs of each hen are hatched in a little basket or bag together.

A record is kept of the number of eggs set, the number infertile, and the number of good chicks which hatch. As each chick is taken from the basket or bag, a numbered wing band is attached to a wing and this number recorded. This wing band serves as the permanent identification of that chick. All of the wing-band numbers of the chicks from each hen are recorded together on one sheet as a family.

Then when the chicks are examined for the various desired characteristics, either for egg production or meat production, it will be found that some hens have produced a much higher percentage of good, desirable chicks than other hens. It is from these good families that breeding birds should be selected in order to make the most rapid improvement.

In pedigree matings, the birds are mated in pens with around 12 to 15 hens and one male in each pen. In this way, both the male and female parent of each chick will be known, and it will be found that there is also great variation in the quality of the chicks produced by the various male birds.

From this brief summary, it is obvious that worthwhile pedigree breeding requires extensive facilities, a rather large number of birds from which to select, and a large amount of labor for trapnesting, pedigree hatching, and record keeping. Actually, modern breeders work with hundreds of thousands of birds and have large staffs of geneticists, pathologists, and experts in all phases of poultry husbandry, as well as business management. Not the least of their tools is a bank of computers to handle the mass of data.

Without doubt, therefore, the small-flock owner, in town or on a farm, certainly will have the greatest success by depending upon one of the established breeders for his stock, unless he wishes to trapnest and keep a record of the pedigree of each chick purely for his own interest and enlightenment.

For the poultryman who is interested in a more detailed understanding of pedigree breeding, there are several college bulletins and books available.

1.   2.   3.   4.   5.   6.   7.   8.   9.   10.   11.   12.   13.   14.   15.   16.

When it is desirable to identify different broods of chicks either in breeding work or in order to keep separate records on chicks from different sources or of different ages, chicks can be identified by punching a hole in the web of the foot. This chart shows the 16 combinations which may be used to identify 16 different groups of chicks.

BREEDING EXHIBITION BIRDS

Many small-flock owners do carry on breeding activities in order to produce fine breed specimens for exhibition at fairs and poultry shows. Since the requirements for selection in this type of breeding vary with almost each breed and variety, it is not possible to go into detail in a book of this size. Breeders of exhibition birds, and all other breeders as well, should have a copy of the *American Standard of*

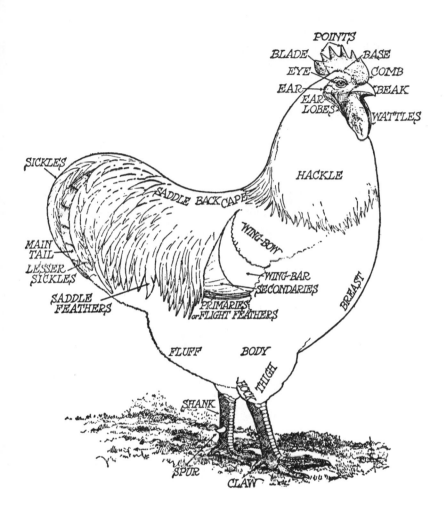

Chart showing names of the principal sections and parts of the body of a male chicken. (*United States Department of Agriculture*)

Perfection, a book published by the American Poultry Association and which describes each of the breeds and varieties for which definite standards have been established in the United States.

In addition to selecting breeding birds according to the Standard, much help can be secured by visiting with other fanciers. More than in any other branch of the poultry business, here will be found the true hobbyist, and at practically any poultry exhibit will be found men willing to discuss at length the good and bad points of the various birds on exhibit and suggest how to make improvements.

The only way to make a start is to visit as many poultry exhibits as possible, study the birds carefully, and finally enter some of your own. By seeing your birds compared with others and asking the judge for his reasons for making his placings, it will be possible to make rather rapid advancement in the breeding and selection of your show birds.

8

Preparation of Poultry and Eggs for Use

Not least in importance is the proper preparation of poultry and eggs for use after they have been produced. Improper preparation nullifies most of the work of production, while knowledge of how to prepare them properly adds to the pleasure of using home-produced chickens and eggs; makes the task of preparation easier; and, if you have surplus products for sale to friends, it enables you to deliver them in attractive, usable form.

KILLING
Killing and dressing chickens is the most complicated task and may be one of the biggest stumbling blocks to the beginner who lives in town, and, therefore, is not accustomed to the slaughter of meat animals, as the farmer is.

If possible, starve the bird to be killed for at least 12 to 24 hours before killing it. It may have water, but withholding food will make the dressing process much easier. Likewise, it is better to have the bird killed and dressed a day or two, or at least several hours, before it is to be cooked. A chicken cooked as soon as it is killed and dressed is likely to be tough and stringy. Like beef, it needs a little aging.

There are various ways of killing a chicken, but along with the killing must be thorough bleeding. A bird which does not bleed completely has a reddened appearance and is not as desirable, not only from the standpoint of appearance, but also from the standpoint of keeping and cooking qualities.

A crude but effective method, probably the best one for the beginner who has an outside chopping block or stump, is to cut off the head with a sharp ax or hatchet. Pull the long wing feathers back and grasp the feathers of both wings and the legs in the left hand. Lay the bird's head on the block and stretch out the neck as far as it can be made to stay. Then, holding the bird firmly in the left hand, cut off its head with a sharp, clean blow. Hold it down over the opposite side of the block until it ceases to struggle and bleeding has stopped. Don't allow the bird to beat its wings against the block or other solid surface. If it does, it may be bruised or even suffer broken wing bones or other damage which will render it unsightly even for home consumption.

The main objection to this method is that blood is likely to be splattered considerably, and it is not suitable for use inside. Sometimes, birds killed in this way do not bleed as well as is desirable.

Another method is to hold the legs and wings as mentioned in the preceding paragraph and grasp the head between the thumb and first finger of the right hand with the top of the head against the palm of the hand. Pull down rather strongly on the head, stretching the neck, and at the same time bending the head back sharply to break the neck. If the neck is stretched properly, the blood vessels break and the blood drains into the loose skin around the neck. The bird will flutter, but no blood will be spilled.

The professional method, which, of course, can be used by anyone, but which requires more practice before proficiency is attained is to use a killing knife to "stick" and bleed the bird. The chicken is suspended head downward at a convenient height by means of a cord with a small block of wood on one end and fastened around both legs or by fastening the legs in a wire shackle.

With the head held in the left hand so that the back of the head is away from the operator and the mouth of the bird open, insert the knife through the mouth and sever the jugular vein at the point shown in the accompanying illustration.

After bleeding is well started, the bird can be killed by sticking the blade through the groove in the roof of the mouth to the back lobe of the brain, as shown in the second illustration. This is not necessary, however, unless the bird is to be dry-picked, which few poultrymen will want to do.

The jugular veins can also be cut from the outside much more easily and this is the method of killing used professionally. It also is recommended for home use.

Grasp the head of the bird in the left hand. Hold it firmly. With a sharp knife, cut the throat just where the head joins the neck. Make the cutting stroke from the side—just above the eye and ear—around to about the middle of the front of the neck. Hold the head for a few seconds to be sure the blood begins to flow freely. If it doesn't, draw the knife around a second time.

It is best to attach a blood cup to the mouth of the bird to hold it in position and also to catch the blood. Blood cups can be purchased or can be made very easily by placing a little concrete, a lead weight, or heavy stones in the bottom of No. 3 cans. A wire is fastened to one edge of the can and bent to form a hook which can be inserted through the mouth.

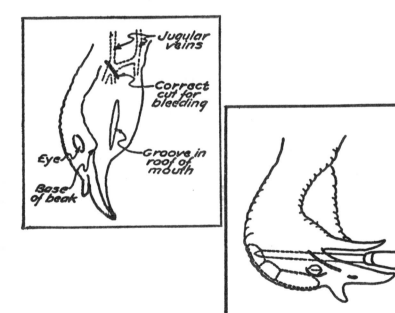

The drawing at the left shows the correct place to cut the jugular veins for proper bleeding. The cut may be made from either the inside of the mouth or from the outside. The drawing at the right side shows the proper position of the knife to stick the bird if it is to be dry-picked.

PLUCKING

Although it does not produce the most attractive carcass, scalding is the easiest process for removing the feathers. The water temperature for scalding can be anywhere between 150 and 190 degrees Fahrenheit, but the hotter the water the less attractive the dressed carcass is likely to be.

Have enough water in a pail to cover the bird thoroughly. Plunge the bird up and down rather vigorously so that the hot water and steam penetrate to the skin. Keep testing a few of the feathers and when they pluck easily, it is ready to be taken out of the water. Test particularly the tail and large wing feathers for they are most difficult to remove. The cooler the water, the longer it will take to loosen the feathers.

Hang the bird at a convenient height by a rope or wire shackle and remove the feathers, beginning with the tail feathers and large wing feathers, which must be jerked out. The remainder of the feathers can be removed with a slight rubbing or twisting movement, taking care not to tear the skin. A dull knife or a regular pinning knife will be helpful in getting hold of the pin feathers. The hair may be singed off over a gas flame, a can of burning alcohol, or over a burning paper. If paper is used, brown wrapping paper will produce less smoke to discolor the skin. After singeing, rinse the carcass under cold running water, rubbing it with your hands, to remove loose particles.

The animal heat should be removed as quickly as possible by placing the bird in a refrigerator or in a tub of cold water, which "plumps" it as well as cools it. Leave in the water for not more than a half hour. Several hours in a cool room will be required for complete cooling.

A second method is the semi-scald method in which the water is heated to a temperature of only 126 to 130 degrees Fahrenheit, according to the age of the bird. Each bird is immersed in water at this temperature for about 30 seconds. The feathers will not be loosened as completely as when hotter water is used, but the skin will retain more of its natural color and appearance. This method is much better to use when the birds are to be sold or stored.

If it is necessary to delay evisceration for more than a few minutes after a bird is killed (if you are dressing several at one time, for example), place the carcass in cold water to cool it as quickly as possible.

EVISCERATING

Eviscerate the carcasses as soon as possible after they have been plucked. All equipment that may come into contact with the carcass must be kept clean. This is especially important once you begin to eviscerate the bird, as well as during any subsequent handling, including cutting up and packaging.

To begin, cut off the feet at the hock joint and cut off the head, leaving as much of the neck as appears edible, and likewise leaving the loose skin around the neck.

This loose skin can be split down the back and the neck cut off as close to the body as possible. This will require a heavy knife or poultry shears.

The procedure from here on will depend upon how the bird is to be cooked. Broilers, which are to be cooked and served in halves, can be split down the back with shears or a heavy knife, cutting along each side of the backbone. The meat can be stripped from the breastbone and the skin cut in two, leaving two equal halves of the bird. The viscera are removed with the backbone after the vent is encircled with a cut to detach the intestines from the skin.

The heart should have the blood squeezed out of it and should be washed. The liver should be detached from the intestines, being very careful not to cut the green gall bladder. Cut away and discard the gall, which is extremely bitter tasting. The gizzard also should be detached and the outer muscle carefully cut through to the inner lining, after which this muscle can be split apart and the inner sac removed whole. This can be done much more easily if the gizzard is thoroughly cooled first.

Even if the birds are to be cut up for frying, this same procedure still may be followed and continued by cutting the carcass into suitable pieces.

For larger young birds and for hens for stewing or fricasseeing, however, the dressed bird is cut up by removing each leg and thigh as a unit, then cutting the leg and thigh apart at the joint. The wings likewise are removed. Cut into the body cavity just below the rear end of the keel or breastbone, cutting through the juncture of the ribs on both sides. When the shoulders are cut, the breast may be removed and cut into two pieces, as is also the back. Here, too, the viscera may be removed after the breast has been severed from the back. Be sure to cut out the oil gland at the base of the tail.

For roasting, the procedure must be somewhat different, as the viscera must be removed without cutting up the carcass. Before the feet are removed from a roasting chicken, cut down the outside of the shank below the hock joint and remove the tendons. This can be done by inserting a nail under them and pulling steadily. Removal of the tendons is not essential, but does add to the pleasure of eating the drumstick.

Then cut off the legs at the hock joint.

Before the neck is removed, split the skin down the back and pull it away from the neck. The windpipe and passageway to the crop will be noticed as flexible tubes between the neck and skin. Separate these from the skin, then also work the crop loose from the skin. Reaching in through the neck cavity, cut off the windpipe and crop outlet as far into the cavity as possible.

Cut off the neck, leaving the skin attached to the body.

At the rear of the bird make a cut below the keel bone, and about 1½ inches above the vent (with the bird on its back). Insert two fingers through this cut and hold the intestine while a circular cut is made around the vent. Push the vent into the body cavity and remove it through the first cut. Reach into the body cavity then and remove the viscera, preferably by drawing out the gizzard first, followed by the remainder of the visceral organs.

The heart, liver, and gizzard are cleaned as described before.

Reach the hand back into the body cavity and the lungs can be felt as soft, spongy masses between the ribs near the front of the body. These can be removed by running a finger under them.

Remove the oil sac at the base of the tail.

Wash out the inside of the body; put the giblets back in; insert the legs through the two cuts at the rear; fold the neck skin over the back and lock it in place with the wings. The bird can be fixed the same way after it is stuffed and no sewing or trussing will be necessary.

The percentage loss in dressing and eviscerating chickens will vary with the size and finish of the bird, but in a three-pound chicken, the blood and feathers will account for about 10 percent of the live weight. The head, shanks, feet, and inedible viscera will account for another 20 percent, making a total loss of 30 percent. The loss is relatively greater in a small bird than in a large one.

PRESERVING SURPLUS BIRDS

Chickens may be preserved by freezing or canning.

Freezing. Quick-frozen poultry is practically equal to fresh-killed in eating qualities. Only birds of good quality should be frozen and these should be dressed by the semi-scald method. They must be completely cooled, eviscerated, and cleaned. The heart, liver, and gizzard should be wrapped separately, but may be left in the body cavity. The birds may be cut up before freezing if preferred.

Chill carcasses well before freezing them—12 hours in a refrigerator at 40 degrees Fahrenheit or below should be adequate for maximum tenderness.

The birds to be frozen should be packaged in plastic freezer bags. Remove as much air from the bag as possible and seal it tightly. Immersing the bagged chicken in warm water before it is sealed will force out the air and mold the bag to the carcass. A foil wrap also may be used, molding it closely to the shape of the bird and folding the edges in a lock seam. Seal with pressure-sensitive tape.

Cut-up chickens can be frozen in special freezer jars or plastic boxes. If halved birds are to be frozen, put a double layer of freezer wrap between the halves so they can be separated more easily.

Label the package by product and date. It is not satisfactory to hold frozen poultry much more than six months in a home freezer. The storage temperature ought to be at 0 degrees Fahrenheit (−18 degrees Centigrade) or lower.

Whole birds to be roasted should be thawed before cooking them. Others can be started cooking as soon as the pieces can be separated. It is safer to thaw birds in a refrigerator but this takes a longer time than if thawed at room temperature or in cold running water.

Canning. All ages of birds may be frozen satisfactorily, but for canning, the older birds are preferred. Great care must be taken to can properly.

The semi-scald process should be used in dressing birds for canning also. After they are thoroughly cooled, eviscerated, and cleaned, they are ready to be cut up.

In one pan place the legs, thighs, gizzards, and breast. The wishbone is first cut off by cutting downward and forward from the front of the breastbone. Cut off the white meat on each side of the breastbone, giving three pieces of white meat, one with the wishbone, and two free from bones.

In the second pan place the wings, back, shoulders, necks and breastbone after the white meat has been removed.

Thoroughly wash and sterilize the jars to be used. Either pints or quarts are satisfactory. A pint jar will hold the legs, thighs, breast meat, and gizzard from one ordinary size Leghorn hen. Pack the pieces carefully and add one-half teaspoonful of salt to each pint. Some people like to add boiling water to within an inch of the top, but it is usually recommended that no water be added.

The lids and rings are then put in place, but not clamped down or screwed on too tightly at this time. Process them in a pressure cooker 75 minutes at 10 pounds pressure for pints and 90 minutes at 10 pounds for quarts. Let the pressure come back to zero before removing the jars, then clamp or screw the lids down tight.

The chicken also may be fried or roasted before canning.

There are two suggested ways of preparing the backs, wings, shoulders, and breastbones. Cook these in a pressure cooker or boil them until the meat comes off the bones readily. Drain off the fat and broth and let it cool. Remove all of the meat, throwing away most of the skin.

To make creamed chicken, use one-half meat and one-half broth and fat. Process in a pressure cooker the same as for whole or cut-up chicken.

For chicken soup from this stock, the suggested plan is to use one-fourth chicken meat, one-fourth broth and fat, and one-half of vegetables diced to a medium size. Boil this five minutes before putting it in the jars and process pints in a pressure cooker 40 minutes at 10 pounds and quarts 55 minutes at 10 pounds.

EGGS

Eggs, with few exceptions, are of high quality when laid, but they deteriorate rather rapidly if kept in a hot, dry atmosphere. For this reason, the eggs ought to be removed from the nests at least three times a day—about mid-morning, right after noon, and at the end of the day. Not only will this permit quicker cooling, but there is less likelihood of eggs being broken in the nests by the hens, and in the winter there will be less danger of some of the eggs freezing.

After the eggs are gathered, they should be held in a cool place, such as a clean cellar or basement. A storage temperature of around 50 to 60 degrees, with high humidity, is preferable. Eggs absorb odors rather easily and should not be held near such things as kerosene, and onions, or where there are musty odors.

When held under these conditions and used reasonably soon, about the only thing likely to be wrong with eggs will be an occasional blood spot in one. If eggs are being sold at retail, many states require that the eggs be candled to remove these and any other inedible eggs. A simple, home-made candler can be made by taking a rolled-oats box or a tin can and cutting a hole in it a little smaller than an egg. Insert a light bulb of around 40 watts in the can. By holding an egg before this light in a darkened room and turning the egg quickly so that the contents rotate inside the shell, the blood spots can be seen rather easily. If you sell to a dealer, it will not be necessary for you to candle them, but the dealer will grade and candle them and likely will pay you according to size and quality.

When eggs are graded for size, those weighing 2 ounces each, or 24 ounces per dozen, are looked upon as "standard." Of course, when pullets begin laying, the eggs are much smaller than this, but the size will increase gradually, usually reaching an ultimate size of 25 to 30 ounces per dozen. Eggs should average about 24 ounces per dozen when the pullet flock has been laying for 4 or 5 months—sometimes sooner.

After the eggs have been thoroughly cooled, they should be packed in cooled cases with the large end of each egg up. The air cell is in the large end. If packed with this end down, more eggs will be broken. Market eggs as quickly as possible after they are produced, within seven days at the most.

For sale to private customers or through a retail store, the use of special egg cartons holding one dozen will be desirable. These can be secured with attractive printing to help the sale of the eggs.

Eggs sold to customers ought to be graded for size in order to provide a more uniform appearance and in order that the price might be established accordingly. The tentative weight classes on United States consumer grades of eggs are as follows:

U.S. WEIGHT CLASSES FOR CONSUMER GRADES
FOR SHELL EGGS

Size or Weight Class	Minimum Net Weight per Doz. (Ounces)	Minimum Net Weight per 30 Doz. (Pounds)	Minimum Weight for Individual Eggs at Rate per Doz. (Ounces)
Jumbo	30	56	29
Extra Large	27	50$^1/_2$	26
Large	24	45	23
Medium	21	39$^1/_2$	20
Small	18	34	17
Peewee	15	28	—

Suitable scales for weighing eggs are available from poultry supply dealers or mail order houses.

If you wish to grade eggs for interior quality by candling, descriptions of the various grades (which vary somewhat by state and locality) may be secured from local marketing agencies, your state poultry department (see list on page 125) or from the United States Department of Agriculture, Washington, D.C. 20250. As a guide to quality characteristics, however, the U.S. standards for quality of individual shell eggs are given in the accompanying chart. The standards of quality provide three additional qualities for eggs with dirty or broken shells: *dirty*—unbroken, may be dirty; *check*—checked or cracked, but not leaking; *leaker*—broken so contents are leaking.

U.S. STANDARDS OF QUALITY

Quality Factor	AA Quality	A Quality	B Quality	C Quality
SHELL	Clean	Clean	Clean; to slightly stained	Clean; to moderately stained
	Unbroken Practically normal	Unbroken Practically normal	Unbroken May be slightly abnormal	Unbroken May be abnormal
AIR CELL	$1/8$ Inch or less in depth, may show unlimited movement and, may be free or bubbly	$3/16$ Inch or less in depth, may show unlimited movement, and may be free or bubbly	$3/8$ Inch or less in depth, may show unlimited movement, and may be free or bubbly	May be over $3/8$ inch in depth, may show unlimited movement, and may be free or bubbly
WHITE	Clear, firm	Clear, may be reasonably firm	Clear, may be slightly weak	May be weak and watery. Small blood clots or spots may be present*
YOLK	Outline slightly defined, practically free from defects	Outline may be fairly well defined, practically free from defects	Outline may be well defined, may be slightly enlarged and flattened

May show definite but not serious defects | Outline may be plainly visible, may be enlarged and flattened, may show clearly visible germ development but no blood may show. Other serious defects |

*If they are small (aggregating not more than $1/8$ inch in diameter)

If you wish to sell eggs direct to consumers or to such users as restaurants, bakeries, or institutions, be sure to get a copy of your state regulations, as suggested previously. They may differ from the federal requirements and also may include licensing or other state requirements.

PRESERVING EGGS

Occasionally, it may be useful to preserve some eggs for use in time of scarcity. There are several methods by which this can be done. There is not nearly as much freezing of eggs as there is of poultry but it is quite easily done by the following procedure.

1.   Use only clean, high-quality eggs with sound shells. If you want to keep them a few days before freezing, place them in the refrigerator. When ready to freeze them, keep them at room temperature for a couple of hours before breaking them. The white will come out more easily than if the eggs are cold.

2.   Whole eggs may be frozen by breaking them into a bowl and adding *one* of the following—the amounts shown are for one dozen eggs:

Salt—one teaspoon.

Sugar—one-half to one tablespoon.

Light corn syrup—one-half to one tablespoon.

Blend thoroughly by stirring gently with a fork (an eggbeater may be used if care is taken not to whip air into the mixture). Thick albumen and/or chalazae from the eggs may cling to the beater or fork. You may either discard it or blend it into the whole egg.

3.   If you prefer them frozen separately, separate the yolks from the whites, using the eggshell or an egg separator.

4.   For each cup of yolks, add *one* of the same ingredients and at the same rate as listed in paragraph 2. Mix thoroughly as for whole eggs.

5.   The whites need no treatment whatever and may be placed immediately into a container for storage.

6.   The eggs are now ready to package for the freezer. They may be frozen in freezer cartons or in glass jars. Eggs expand on freezing, so leave about an inch of space at the top of the container or they may either force off the lid or break the container.

Label the container with date, product, quantity, and details of treatment. Freeze and store at zero degrees Fahrenheit or lower. They should keep satisfactorily for 6 to 8 months.

They may be thawed in a refrigerator (2 or 3 days) or by putting the unopened container in a pan of cool tap water (6 to 8 hours). Once thawed, keep them refrigerated and use them within 3 to 5 days (the yolks no later then 3). If you want to beat them, bring them to room temperature first.

These thawed yolks and whites may be used just as you now use fresh egg whites and yolks. For convenience, you may use the following figures for estimating the amount of yolk and white corresponding to one egg:

Two tablespoons of white equals the white of one egg

One tablespoon of yolk equals the yolk of one egg

A common method of preserving eggs which has been used for many years is that of putting them in sodium silicate, commonly called water glass, which can be purchased at almost any drugstore very inexpensively. Eggs laid during March, April, and May usually keep better than eggs laid later in the season.

Only fresh eggs with sound, strong shells should be preserved, and any eggs which are soiled, cracked, or even slightly checked should not be used. For 14 to 15 dozen medium-size eggs, use one quart of water glass to nine quarts of water that has been boiled and cooled. Measure the water into a crock or galvanized can of six- to eight-gallon capacity, being sure that the vessel has been thoroughly cleaned and scalded.

Add the water glass and stir the mixture thoroughly. Place the eggs in the water glass solution and be careful to have at least one inch of the solution covering the eggs at all times. If there are not enough eggs on hand when the solution is first made, more eggs may be added from time to time. Keep the solution containing the preserved eggs in a cool, dry place, the closer to refrigerator temperature, the better. Cover the container tightly to prevent evaporation. If kept cool and covered, they can be held for as long as six months.

The eggs should be taken out only for immediate use and should be washed to remove the coating of the solution before the shell is broken. Before preserved eggs are boiled, a pinhole should be made in the large end of the shell to permit air to escape and to prevent the shell from bursting.

PICKLED EGGS

Pickled eggs are hard-cooked eggs that have been soaked in a solution of vinegar, salt, spices, and other seasonings. Some solutions add color to the eggs to brighten snacks or salads.

After the eggs have been hard-cooked and peeled, pack one dozen medium-sized eggs loosely in a quart jar so the container will hold plenty of pickling solution. Any container that can be sealed tightly is satisfactory.

Pour the hot pickling solution over the eggs; seal the container; put it into the refrigerator immediately. Keep in the refrigerator while seasoning. It takes at least one week to season small eggs adequately, and from two to four weeks for normal and larger eggs. You can keep pickled eggs several months in the pickling solution at refrigerator temperature. Drain before serving.

There are many recipes for pickling solutions; with experience, you might even concoct one of your own. The two recipes below are from a pamphlet of the University of Wisconsin Extension Service, from which these instructions were adapted also. Heat the mixture to near boiling and simmer for five minutes before pouring it over the eggs. Both recipes are for one quart of pickled eggs.

Red Beet Eggs	*Dilled Eggs*
1 cup red-beet juice	$1^{1}/_{2}$ cups white vinegar
$1^{1}/_{2}$ cup cider vinegar	1 cup water
1 teaspoon brown sugar	$^{3}/_{4}$ teaspoon dill seed
A few small canned red	$^{1}/_{4}$ teaspoon white pepper
beets (can be sliced)	3 teaspoons salt
	$^{1}/_{4}$ teaspoon mustard seed
	$^{1}/_{2}$ teaspoon onion juice
	$^{1}/_{2}$ teaspoon minced garlic

Poultry and eggs are among the finest foods, providing proteins of high quality, minerals and vitamins. In fact, egg proteins are of such high quality that they are used as the standard by which other proteins are compared. They contain all of the essential amino acids.

Two eggs supply an impressive percentage of the daily requirement of essential nutrients—an average of 10 to 30 percent for adults. Eggs are also recognized as an especially rich source of high-quality protein, unsaturated fats, iron, phosphorus, trace minerals, vitamins A, E, and K, and all B vitamins, including vitamin B_{12}. Eggs are second only to fish-liver oils as a natural source of vitamin D. Although eggs are low in calcium (present in the shell) and contain little or no vitamin C, when they are eaten with milk and citrus fruits all essential nutrients are supplied.

It is only good business, therefore, for poultry producers, even those operating on a small scale, to promote use of their products at every opportunity. More information, including recipe leaflets are available from the following organizations:

Eggs. American Egg Board, 205 Touhy Avenue, Park Ridge, Illinois 60068.

Broilers. National Broiler Council, 1155 15th Street NW, Washington, D.C. 20005.

Turkeys. National Turkey Federation, Suite 302, Reston International Center, Reston, Virginia 22091.

Ducklings. National Duckling Council, 2 North Riverside Plaza, Chicago, Illinois 60606.

9

How to Expand

If you have been reasonably successful with a small flock of chickens, sooner or later you are practically certain to wonder about the possibility of getting into the poultry business on a larger scale. This is a logical thought, and in this chapter an endeavor will be made to outline some of the things to take into consideration in reaching a decision.

The first consideration is, do you like chickens and are you willing to put in long hours of hard work caring for them? Unless you can honestly answer yes, you probably might just as well stop thinking about it. While it might be possible to make a fair financial success with poultry even though you do not like the work, the chances are decidedly against it. Furthermore, life is too short to spend it in struggling with a business from which you derive no pleasure.

While your location need not necessarily be the determining factor, it should be considered. It will be easier to establish a successful poultry farm if there are other such farms in your area. A community in which poultry raising is a major interest usually will have better facilities for providing the feed, equipment, and other supplies needed; will have better market outlets; and there will be a greater opportunity for sharing information and experiences, which always is helpful. Poultry raising has developed much more extensively in some communities or whole states than in others, usually due to economic factors such as favorable climate, availability of feed, or nearness to good markets. Sometimes a community may develop considerable interest in poultry because some one leader has been successful and others follow his lead.

On the other hand, successful poultry farms will be found in isolated sections which may not appear, at first glance, to have any of these advantages. As a rule, such poultrymen have been willing to produce a product well above the average in quality and have devoted a portion of their time to developing a market, either wholesale or at retail, which will pay in proportion to that quality.

CITY POULTRYMEN

Many people who have been successful with a small backyard flock of chickens in town have a desire to get out on a small farm where they not only may produce a larger share of their food, but may even expand the poultry enterprise to the point where it will be their principal occupation. Whether this move should be made is a harder problem to answer, for it may involve a rather drastic change in living habits, as well as in work. It is one thing to be successful with a small hobby when one is not dependent upon it for a living, and quite another to give up an established occupation for one in which there is a considerable element of chance.

There is a middle step, of course, in which a family may move to a small acreage on which the poultry enterprise, as well as other enterprises, may be built up while retaining the old occupation in town. Many people find this the most delightful manner of living, especially where there are several children who can help with the work. At the same time, the children are benefited by having regular work to do and by the more wholesome environment usually found in the country.

This, undoubtedly, would be the best procedure when finances do not permit building up the farm to a self-sustaining basis right away. In such cases, it is better to start with a small flock which can be handled easily, then if something does go wrong, there will be no great loss. The flock can be expanded as you grow in knowledge and experience, and as you are financially able.

One point in this connection is that if a plan of management is giving success, do not be hasty in changing it. Do not overlook possible ways of saving labor or increasing efficiency, but do not be so eager to adopt new ideas that you neglect fundamental principles of good poultry management, such as the following:

1. There will be considerable variation from year to year in return for labor and management due to changes in costs (primarily for feed) and in the market price of eggs. These fluctuations cannot be eliminated but they may be minimized by good management in buying and in marketing.

2. High egg production per hen is absolutely essential for high cash return. The National Research Council has published a table showing that a 4-pound hen requires about 56 pounds of feed merely to maintain herself for a year without producing any eggs. It will take another 15 pounds for her to produce the first 100 eggs; 13 pounds to produce the second 100; and 14 pounds to produce the third 100. For the first 100 eggs, the total feed consumption was 8.58 pounds per dozen; 5.08 pounds per dozen for 200 eggs; and only 3.96 pounds per dozen for 300 eggs.

3. High production in the fall months is even more important than high annual egg production. It follows, however, that those poultrymen who get high fall egg production also have high annual production. If you are serving retail markets, you will need to strive for an even flow of eggs throughout the year. If you are selling eggs wholesale, you probably will be ahead if you produce a greater volume of eggs from July 1 to January 1 than from January 1 to July 1.

4. Low hen mortality is absolutely necessary for high cash returns. Mortality can be reduced by getting birds of good breeding, following good brooding and rearing practices, and using good feeding and management practices with the laying flock.

5. Regardless of the type or volume of poultry business, a high gross cash earning in proportion to the investment is essential. A substantial part of the total investment must be in houses and equipment that will return a large cash income. Your goal might be at least one dollar of sales for each dollar invested.

6. Labor efficiency on poultry farms varies tremendously with the equipment, layout, volume of business, and with the poultryman himself. Efficiency of labor may be measured in terms of gross sales for each dollar of labor cost, including the owner's. It may also be measured in terms of the number of laying hens kept per man.

7. Volume of business is one of the most important requirements on a poultry farm. Investment in the farm, the home, and the service buildings is much the same regardless of the volume of business. Extra investment in laying houses, livestock, and equipment for developing

various possible sources of income add greatly to the gross cash sales without a proportionate increase in cost.

8. Quite often a poultryman shows efficient management in one part of the business, while other parts are neglected or inefficiently managed. The number of the above factors efficiently managed has a very definite relationship to labor income.

RECORDS

It will not be possible to compare your poultry project with these or similar figures unless accurate records are kept. Most small-flock owners like to keep records for the interesting facts which they reveal. But when the poultry flock is expanded, records become vitally necessary as a means of determining whether the flock is returning a profit or losing money, and why. Records also are necessary for the accurate preparation of income tax returns.

For the small flock, a very simple record system will suffice. The poultry department at Purdue University suggests the following form for the monthly and annual records. The daily records can be kept in a small notebook or on a calendar.

Somewhat more elaborate records will be needed for larger flocks.

Practically all farm-management specialists now suggest that a farmer, instead of just "keeping a few chickens," decide definitely what he wants to accomplish with his flock and determine its size accordingly. If the only interest in chickens is to provide eggs and meat for the family, and sales are merely incidental, there is little reason why a farmer should have any larger flock than the town poultry raiser who keeps a backyard flock for the same reason. Certainly two or three dozen hens will be ample. Even this small flock, of course, should be of good breeding and have good housing and care, or else it will be cheaper to buy the eggs and poultry for the family.

But the farmer who looks to his chickens to provide a part of the profit of the farm enterprise should give serious consideration indeed to expanding the flock to a size which will be most efficient and profitable.

At one time, the recommended increase in size was from the home flock up to a few hundred birds. That is seldom practical now because of limited marketing facilities for small quantities of eggs. Egg buyers want eggs in volume. Nor can such a flock hold good direct markets to food stores, restaurants, and similar institutions because of grading requirements and a lack of a uniform supply of the desired sizes throughout the year. As a rule, the market for these flocks of a few hundred birds is limited to individual customers and to small-volume

FRESH EGGS ARE PERISHABLE ~ ~ WATCH THE TEMPERATURE

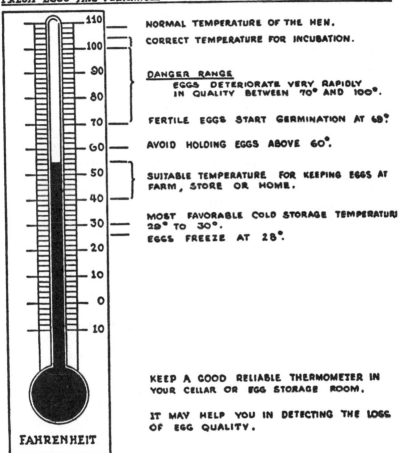

NORMAL TEMPERATURE OF THE HEN.

CORRECT TEMPERATURE FOR INCUBATION.

DANGER RANGE
EGGS DETERIORATE VERY RAPIDLY
IN QUALITY BETWEEN 70° AND 100°.

FERTILE EGGS START GERMINATION AT 68°.

AVOID HOLDING EGGS ABOVE 60°.

SUITABLE TEMPERATURE FOR KEEPING EGGS AT FARM, STORE OR HOME.

MOST FAVORABLE COLD STORAGE TEMPERATURE 29° TO 30°.
EGGS FREEZE AT 28°.

KEEP A GOOD RELIABLE THERMOMETER IN YOUR CELLAR OR EGG STORAGE ROOM.

IT MAY HELP YOU IN DETECTING THE LOSS OF EGG QUALITY.

FAHRENHEIT

The necessary information relating to temperature and the proper handling of eggs is summarized on this "thermometer." In addition to a cool temperature, a high humidity is desirable.

egg users. Even here, the state grading regulations may be a problem.

Thus, in speaking of expanding, we are thinking in terms of thousands of hens instead of hundreds. Even then, the first thing to investigate is market. Of course, as a larger-flock owner you may also like to sell your eggs direct to customers who come to your farm or to whom you deliver. This is not a very efficient method of marketing, however, and supply and demand may not always be in balance. But producers who like to deal with people and who can get a premium for their eggs do well at direct marketing.

In many areas, it is no longer a simple matter to find a wholesale egg buyer. Such buyers are interested in volume, quality, and dependability. In the modern food business, the egg dealer must make firm commitments to his store, restaurant, hospital, and other customers so he must have the same dependability of supply from his producers.

BUILDINGS AND EQUIPMENT

In making this kind of expansion, you will want to consider using the cage system of housing and managing hens. There are several cage systems, differing in design and arrangement of the cages. Perhaps your first step in evaluating the different systems is to attend one of the state or national poultry expositions where the various makes of equipment are on display. Your county agent or poultry-supply dealer can tell you of these expositions. Follow up by visiting some poultrymen and getting the benefit of their experience. You are proposing a major move which justifies some investigation and study.

An important consideration at this point is to get a poultry house unit in which the building and equipment are coordinated. It isn't wise to order one and then the other independently. If you do order one without consideration of the other, you may find that the cage system you want does not fit well into the house you have ordered.

If you decide to stay with the floor system of housing, you will want to consider carefully the different systems of automatic feeding and watering, nesting arrangements, and provisions for manure removal and storage. Availability of prompt servicing of the equipment should be a consideration also.

BREEDS

As long as the poultry is merely a hobby, the breed and variety of chickens kept is not too important, for the pleasure derived from them is a large part of the compensation. When the flock is enlarged, however, and expected to pay a profit, then the breed, and particularly the breeding back of the strain purchased, is extremely important. If you are interested primarily in egg production and your market prefers white eggs, then the Leghorn-type strains, already referred to, definitely are preferred.

If you are interested in both meat and high egg production, particularly if white eggs do not return any premium on your market, then one of the more common American breeds, such as Rhode Island Reds, New Hampshires, White Plymouth Rocks, or Barred Plymouth Rocks, should be chosen. Crossbred birds, produced by crossing two separate breeds, also are very popular in many sections. Careful crossing of good strains frequently produces birds which grow somewhat faster and feather quicker than their purebred parents. Some breeders also offer brown-egg strain crosses bred for high egg production in the same manner as the Leghorn-type. But the Leghorn-type birds are almost universally used for commercial egg production in the United States.

FINANCING

Suppose you have decided you would like to expand your flock, but lack the necessary finances. After all, it does require a considerable investment in buildings, equipment, stock, and feed before there is any return, and a still larger investment is required for land and a home if you are moving from town to a farm.

It is desirable to keep the investment as low as possible, but, of course, it must be sufficient to provide the necessary land (if you don't have it already), suitable buildings, and good stock. There will be considerable variation in investment needed in different sections of the country due to differences in climatic requirements and building costs.

When one begins with a small flock and expands gradually, the total investment is not required at the beginning. On the other hand, some additional capital above the first investment will be required to meet operating costs.

For either the original investment or for operating capital, it may be necessary to seek a loan. There are numerous sources of loans for the sound expansion of a farm enterprise or the purchase of a new farm. Local banks, and building and loan associations are among the first such institutions to be considered.

In purchasing a farm, however, it usually is desirable to finance the loan over a long term of years, and it is well to be sure that the terms of the loan are fitted to your needs. The Farm Credit Administration has available some very excellent bulletins on the various types of loans and the proper use of credit, either for purchasing a farm or for expanding production. These bulletins may be secured by addressing the Farm Credit Administration of the district serving your state. Cities in which these district offices are located and the states which they serve are as follows:

Springfield, Massachusetts—Connecticut, Maine, Massachusetts, New Hampshire, New Jersey, New York, Rhode Island, and Vermont.

Baltimore, Maryland—Delaware, District of Columbia, Maryland, Pennsylvania, Virginia, and West Virginia.

Columbia, South Carolina—Florida, Georgia, North Carolina, and South Carolina.

Louisville, Kentucky—Indiana, Kentucky, Ohio, and Tennessee.

New Orleans, Louisiana—Alabama, Louisiana, and Mississippi.

St. Louis, Missouri—Arkansas, Illinois, and Missouri.

St. Paul, Minnesota—Michigan, Minnesota, North Dakota, and Wisconsin.

Omaha, Nebraska—Iowa, Nebraska, South Dakota, and Wyoming.

Wichita, Kansas—Colorado, Kansas, New Mexico, and Oklahoma.

Houston, Texas—Texas.

Berkeley, California—Arizona, California, Hawaii, Nevada, and Utah.

Spokane, Washington—Idaho, Alaska, Montana, Oregon, and Washington.

These bulletins, as well as additional information on loans, may be secured also by local contacts with units of the Farm Credit Administration. These may be made through the secretary of the National Farm Loan Association serving your county if you are interested in buying a farm. If you wish a loan for operating expenses, then the secretary-treasurer of the Production Credit Association serving your county should be consulted. If you do not know where these are located, the county agricultural agent in most instances will be able to direct you.

CONTRACTING

If you are in an area where large-scale poultry and egg production is not a common enterprise, there may be difficulty in finding financing simply because lending agencies are not familiar with poultry operations.

In that event, you may want to look into the possibility of contracting your production in return for financial help and management counsel. Among those who may be interested in entering into such a contract are feed companies, breeders, and wholesale egg buyers. Such contracting arrangements have been developed as a means of sharing the risk and the profit, and may be especially attractive to the person who lacks confidence or experience.

Poultry and farm management specialists at the University of Wisconsin have outlined four types of egg production contracts and have listed some items which should be checked before entering into such a contract. The following material has been adapted from their report. I would emphasize again their suggestion that you fully understand the terms and conditions of the agreement, and the responsibilities of each of you, before signing the contract.

A. *A fixed fee per dozen eggs.*

The producer furnishes housing, equipment, labor, utilities and sometimes litter and receives a payment of 4 to 7 cents per dozen eggs produced. Other parties furnish ready-to-lay hens, feed, medication, and own all eggs as well as the salvage hens at the end of the production period. Some contracts of this type also pay bonuses for good feed conversion, high percentage of salable eggs or low mortality.

B. *A fixed fee per hen per month.*

The producer furnishes the same items as in *A* but receives a payment of from 7 to 13 cents per hen per month. Bonuses or incentive payments may be added as in *A*.

C. *Percentage of returns.*

The producer furnishes the items listed in *A* and receives a percentage of total egg returns (usually 15 to 18 percent). The feed supplier usually receives 50 to 55 percent of the return while the supplier of ready-to-lay pullets gets 26 to 28 percent and usually retains ownership of the birds. The percentage received by any party must be proportional to his contribution in the form of material and/or services. This contract has the built-in incentive of increasing returns by doing a better job. This is the only type of contract that treats all parties proportionately as both input and output prices change.

D. *Guaranteed-price agreement.*

The producer agrees to supply eggs of a designated grade in a given volume for a guaranteed price. The producer in this case usually supplies all inputs (housing, pullets, feed, etc.). He is protected against price declines but cannot benefit from market price increases. Generally, this type of contract does not endure for continued renewals because the guaranteed price is usually set slightly below market averages.

Egg contracting makes legal partners of the producer and his suppliers or marketing agent. To be successful, each must have the utmost trust and confidence in the other. Since the contract is a binding financial agreement, all details must be clearly stated. Each party must see an advantage in the contract approach; it must serve a purpose.

Contracting in egg production allows all segments of the industry to schedule their programs well in advance, thereby effecting economies of supply and helping to prevent market gaps or overloads. This approach allows the producer to calculate his return with less dependence upon day-to-day price fluctuations. Generally, it tends to lessen selling costs and improve service. Under contract arrangements the producer gives up the right to claim all of the profit, but by so doing gains one or more partners in the sharing of risk.

Check these points before entering on egg production contract:

1.   Who keeps the books?

2.   Who is responsible for services (obtaining diagnosis, recommending management changes, prescribing medication, etc.)?

3.   Who removes the birds?

4.   Who is responsible for clean-out and when?

5.   Who pays for medication and at what price (retail or other)?

6.   What is the length of the contract; how may it be extended, terminated or renewed?

7.   What is the extent of liability of each party? (This is a legal point you should cover with your attorney.)

8.   What is the interval between groups of birds when the house will be empty and hence not a source of income?

9.   What is the age, breeding and rearing program of replacement stock?

10.   What are the conditions of egg collection (storage and delivery or pickup)?

11.   Is there any allowance for eggs (undergrade or otherwise) used in the producer's household?

12.   Are the total contributions (goods and services) of each of the participants listed?

Some contracting arrangements offer a package deal which includes house, equipment, pullets, feed—virtually everything needed to make a going operation. But the financing load may not leave you much, if any, profit and it would be well to visit other producers who have operated under the same or similar contracts and learn of their experiences.

SOURCES OF INFORMATION

In this connection, it may be helpful to list some of the possible sources of information and help which are available to poultry raisers in most communities. These will include the hatcheryman, feed dealer, the vocational agriculture teacher found in the high school of most towns and small cities, the county agricultural agent located in the county seat (he is known as the farm adviser in some states), the field man of loan agencies, such as the Farm Credit Administration or Farm Security Administration, the poultry department and extension poultrymen at the state agricultural college (see list below). The state agricultural experiment station is in connection with the college in practically all states. Then, of course, there is the United States Department of Agriculture, Washington, D.C. The United States Department of Agriculture and the various state colleges issue numerous bulletins covering specific phases of poultry management. A postcard request to the United States Department of Agriculture or to your state college will bring a list of the bulletins currently available. It will be worthwhile to add many of these to your poultry library.

Do not overlook the many helpful booklets issued by equipment manufacturers, feed companies, pharmaceutical companies, and others. Many of these present sound, detailed information along specific lines and can be very helpful to poultrymen.

Several times I have referred to state poultry specialists and poultry departments. Not all colleges of agriculture have a department of poultry science but all will have someone equipped to reply to your queries. If you don't know the name of an individual, simply address Extension Poultry Specialist, College of Agriculture (except where noted otherwise) at the following locations, listed by state.

AGRICULTURAL COLLEGES AND EXPERIMENT STATIONS IN THE UNITED STATES AND CANADA

UNITED STATES

Alabama: Auburn 36830
Alaska: Palmer 99645
Arizona: Tucson 85721
Arkansas: Fayetteville 72701
California: Davis 95616
Colorado: Fort Collins 80521
Connecticut: Storrs 06268
Delaware: Newark 19711
Florida: Gainesville 32601
Georgia: Athens 30601
Hawaii: Honolulu 96822
Idaho: Moscow 83843
Illinois: Urbana 61803

Indiana: Lafayette 47907
Iowa: Ames 50010
Kansas: Manhattan 66502
Kentucky: Lexington 40506
Louisiana: Baton Rouge 70803
Maine: Orono 04473
Maryland: College Park 20742
Massachusetts: Amherst 01002
Michigan: East Lansing 48823
Minnesota: St. Paul 55101
Mississippi: State College 39762
Missouri: Columbia 65202
Missouri: (Poultry Experiment Station) Mountain Grove 65711
Montana: Bozeman 59715
Nebraska: Lincoln 68503
Nevada: Reno 89507
New Hampshire: Durham 03824
New Jersey: New Brunswick 08903
New Mexico: State College 88001
New York: Ithaca 14850
North Carolina: Raleigh 27607
North Dakota: Fargo 58102
Ohio: Columbus 43210
Ohio: (Experiment Station) Wooster 44691
Oklahoma: Stillwater 74074
Oregon: Corvallis 97331
Pennsylvania: State College 16802
Rhode Island: Kingston 02881
South Carolina: Clemson 29631
South Dakota: Brookings 57006
Tennessee: Knoxville 37901
Texas: College Station 77843
Utah: Logan 84321
Vermont: Burlington 05401
Virginia: Blacksburg 24061
Washington: Pullman 99163
Washington: (Western Washington Experiment Station) Puyallup
    98421
West Virginia: Morgantown 26506
Wisconsin: Madison 53706
Wyoming: Laramie 82070
United States Department of Agriculture, Washington, D.C. 20250.

CANADA

Alberta: Edmonton
British Columbia: Vancouver
Manitoba: Winnipeg
Nova Scotia: Truro
Ontario: Guelph
Quebec: Macdonald College, Macdonald College
Saskatchewan: Saskatoon
Dominion Department of Agriculture, Ottawa

IO

The Hobby Side of the Poultry Industry

The production of meat and eggs is the economic basis for the poultry industry. There is another area of poultry interest—the fancy—that has a considerable number of devoted followers who raise various breeds and varieties of chickens for their excellence of shape and color.

There are more than 300 different combinations of physical features and color patterns. Each represents a particular shape, size or color and each transmits these general characteristics to its offspring so long as they are mated to their own kind. To get the full picture of this side of poultry, one must do two things. First, be aware of the background of the poultry industry and how it evolved. Second, visit a poultry show to get a visual picture of the many beautiful colors and unique forms that exist in the poultry world. It also helps to see the enthusiasm with which many of the exhibitors pursue their hobby.

THE BACKGROUND

In the first half of the nineteenth century, the poultry population of the United States was highly varied. Coming from many sources, the chickens were mainly dark-colored and medium-sized. Within any given community there tended to be a similarity because the most successful poultry raiser was the source of the breeding males for many other flocks.

Importations of other types of chickens began in the 1830s and 40s, adding to the variation of the poultry population. Many claims were being made about the worth of these new arrivals and of chickens in general. The founding of farm journals and the appearance of poultry books pointed toward the need for an accepted method of identifying the great array of poultry shapes and colors.

This need was climaxed at the first poultry show in the United States, held in Boston in 1849. Chickens were presented to the judges by the hundreds for evaluation. How were they to be judged and who was to say what the proper sizes and colors should be? Obviously, a standard of identification was needed. The same problems were arising in Great Britain, where a gentleman had devised a guide or book of standards. Although the book was brought to the United States, it was not readily accepted because it was thought to represent the arbitrary standards of a single person.

While agreement was not easily reached, the Boston Poultry Show did accomplish one thing—it received a lot of coverage in the press. Among the exhibitors was Daniel Webster. In covering him, the press popularized poultry raising among the professional class and soon doctors, lawyers, and clergymen were raising "good" chickens, giving poultry a dignity it had not previously enjoyed. It also enhanced the demand for shows and this furthered the need for accepted standards.

It was with this in mind that a group of poultrymen met in Buffalo, New York in 1873 and organized the American Poultry Association. They proceeded immediately to compile and print the *American Standard of Excellence*. Using democratic procedures and drawing upon the collective opinions of breeders, *American Standard* received the acceptance that the British Standard had not. The name was later changed to *American Standard of Perfection*. It has been repeatedly revised and enlarged but continues today to serve as the guide by which all domestic poultry in the United States is identified. It also is the technical reference used by judges in placing awards at shows.

The A.P.A. licenses persons to act as judges. The licensing is based upon the person's knowledge of the over 300 breeds and varieties described in the *Standard of Perfection*.

THE SHOW

The poultry show is an organized presentation and evaluation (by comparison) of the various breeds and varieties entered for exhibit. Each bird is held in a separate wire coop. Individuals are grouped in classes according to age and sex within each variety. Each class is placed, using the *Standard of Perfection* as a guide.

A best-of-variety is then selected for competition with the other variety winners for best of breed, then continuing in the pyramid fashion up through breed groups until the over-all champions are decided. The process is orderly but takes time because of the steps involved. This adds to the suspense and the over-all effect is as exciting as the competition afforded by any other sport.

The winners represent a combination of breeding, conditioning and knowledge, which reflects the owner's touch. This is why success in the showroom is often likened to an art, whereas success in the commercial poultry world may more likely be due to the application of science.

WHO SHOWS POULTRY?

Poultry exhibitors come from all walks of life and from virtually every age group. Success in a profession or in the business world does not guarantee success in the showroom. Many of the consistent winners in shows have minimal education and hold very ordinary jobs but they understand chickens and how to breed and condition them. They are also willing to devote the time and effort required to bring the desired response from the birds.

Young people often take up the breeding of fancy poultry as a challenge. They seek to move more rapidly toward perfection of shape and color and sometimes the drive of youth is successful.

Regardless of age or wealth, a win carries the thrill and prestige that is accorded the winner in any sport and since the poultry fancy contains such a wide array of ages and social levels among its devotees, it is truly an equalizer. There is no generation gap among people of a common interest and this becomes readily evident to the spectator at a poultry show.

Because chickens are very adaptable creatures, they can be kept under a variety of circumstances. Also, because they have a reasonably low unit value (as contrasted with other animals) many people are able to engage in the hobby of poultry raising where space and/or finances would not permit them to raise purebred horses or other large animals. Breeding fancy poultry offers the raiser an opportunity to sense the accomplishment of coming even closer to the ideal by his own genetic selection.

The people who are active in the fancy poultry hobby fall generally into three categories. They are:

1.   Those who truly love the birds and enjoy their company. They study the various breeds and make a concerted effort to improve

them. To them the bird comes first and the show is sort of the "frosting on the cake." While they enjoy participation in the show, they would raise their favorites if no show existed.

2. The poultry curious. These people enjoy having as many different kinds of chickens (and other fowl) as they can obtain. The shows offer them an opportunity to see new varieties and make contact with other people of similar interest. These individuals rarely accomplish much improvement in quality of their stocks because of limited numbers of each but do a real service in keeping some of the rare varieties alive and before the public.

3. The social poultryman. Here we find persons who use their exhibition poultry as an excuse to participate in the social aspect of the shows and the organizations that sponsor them. They frequently purchase their birds ready to show, which enables them to become involved much more quickly than if they were to wait for their own chicks to hatch and grow into show-age birds. These people enter and leave the poultry fancy frequently. Their orientation is with people, not birds, whereas the other two groups, especially the bird lovers, are much more permanently attached to their birds and leave the fancy only under extreme circumstances and with deep regrets.

Superimposed over all three groups is the intrigue of do-it-yourself or personal innovation. The design and construction of transport coops, incubators, buildings, and equipment offers a particular fascination for many persons. Sophisticated homemade systems for control of temperature, light, and water supply are common among the fanciers who really care. Mechanical exercise devices, strategically positioned vision openings, elevated feed containers, dust filters and an almost endless list of personal inventions frequently grace the poultry quarters of the more advanced fanciers.

TRADING OR SALES

Most shows emphasize the sales value of a win. Many exhibitors purchase breeding stock that wins at a show or obtain birds from the flock that produced the winner. This builds a business value into showing. As further encouragement, many shows provide a section where birds may be displayed and offered for sale or trade. Since these birds are not entered in the competition they can be removed from the showroom as soon as a deal has been closed.

The sale section provides additional income to show management from the rental of the sale coops. It also tends to increase the attendance at shows since many people are reluctant to price winning birds for fear the quotation may be beyond their means. The sale sections frequently contain birds that are too young to show to a good advantage in the competitive classes or are out of condition because of age, physical damage, or sterility. They may also be birds that have been declared surplus by their owners for a variety of reasons, including some of those above.

PRIZES AND AWARDS

There was a time when prizes or awards of cash were given by municipal governments to encourage or reward quality or excellence. With the movement of poultry raising toward the totally economic emphasis on meat and eggs, public financial support of poultry shows has largely disappeared. State fairs and a few county fairs still pay cash premiums but the bulk of the fancy poultry shows award ribbons and trophies. Cash prizes are limited to special champion awards in some shows and are completely absent in others. This has somewhat divided exhibitor participation.

The county and state fairs are held in late summer and early fall, when many current year birds are very immature and old birds are in their natural seasonal molt. Fanciers are therefore reluctant to show their birds because they are not in the most presentable condition.

The people who exhibit at these fairs are generally showing to collect systematically the premium money offered in exchange for presenting reasonably acceptable specimens to the public for viewing much in the same way they might view a zoo. The display is acceptable to the general public but lacks the finesse sought by the fancier at the exhibition-type shows. The latter are generally held in late fall and early winter when birds, both young and old, are in a better state of feather.

FINANCING THE SHOWS

The main source of revenue for the exhibition poultry show is the entry fee or coop rental. In addition, ads are frequently sold in the show announcement or premium list and donations of trophies and other awards are solicited from club members and local merchants.

The shows are usually staged or sponsored by local or regional organizations of poultry fanciers. The clubs usually conduct their shows annually on a set date such as the first weekend in October or the first Saturday in December. By adhering to the same dates each year, it becomes possible for exhibitors to plan a schedule of participation that includes several shows each year. In many instances, participation becomes an outing in which wives and children become involved. They look forward to meeting the families of other fanicers each year as they take in a circuit of exhibitions.

ORGANIZATIONS

The parent organization of the fancy poultry interest continues to be the American Poultry Association. In the early part of the twentieth century, it was joined by the American Bantam Association, an organization formed to serve the particular interests of those who were breeding the miniatures. Today both organizations publish a book of standards (*Standard of Perfection*), license judges, and publish established procedures for conducting shows. Each organization has a board of directors reflecting geographic distribution and each has a representative in nearly every state.

Every year both organizations hold a meeting and show in connection with some local poultry show. Both are not usually held in conjunction with the same show. The selection of these annual shows is on a somewhat rotational basis and in this way they move about the country.

In addition to the two national organizations, there are many state and local clubs, as well as several organizations which serve the interest of a single breed or variety. These "specialty clubs" usually stage an annual show hosted by some local show. Specialty clubs also serve to advise the the A.P.A. and the A.B.A. when changes in the standard for the breed are desired by the persons who breed and exhibit them.

THE EFFECTS OF SOCIETY

Until the 1930s, backyard poultry flocks were very common in rural, village, and city locations. Many were of specific breeds and a considerable number of their owners competed at local poultry shows. Nearly every town of any size had an annual poultry show.

As the emphasis of the industry moved toward specialized egg production in the 1920s, the shows began to decline. The decline was hastened by the depression of the 1930s and the ready availability of day-old baby chicks from the developing hatchery industry. The purchase of mass-produced baby chicks eliminated the need to continue mating and hatching from many flocks. This lessened the demand for breeding males—one of the principle sale products from many of the local purebred flocks.

The future of the backyard flock was further dimmed in the 1940s when many cities and villages passed ordinances prohibiting the keeping of poultry. People who had held on to a few representatives of recognized breeds were then forced to discontinue keeping them. The disintegration of the base of potential exhibitors resulted in a marked reduction of the number poultry shows. A few of the poultry enthusiasts who could no longer keep birds took to collecting books and magazines about them. Collecting "poultry paper" continues today as another facet of the poultry hobby.

The desire of many people to move to the country from central city areas has brought with it renewed interest in the home poultry flock. Producing some of the family's own food has strong appeal when reports of higher prices and impending shortages are in the news almost daily. Some new producers not only want to produce their own eggs and table fowl but also find the hatching of chicks and mating of fowls additional points of interest. 4-H clubs and other youth groups have incorporated these experiences into biology programs. Many of the people who are interested in this aspect are intrigued by the unusual and find the Crested Polish or the black-skinned Silkie even more interesting than the typical commercial egg layer.

The result has been a marked increase in attendance at, and participation in, shows. The number of shows is again on the increase, causing a considerable rise in the numbers of some of the rare and unusual breeds. One- and two-day weekend shows are commonplace. Locating the show site where motor homes and camping trailers can be hooked up has made the poultry show an integral part of a family camping weekend for many households.

The Society for the Preservation of Poultry Antiquities has been founded to encourage the breeding of the rare varieties and prevent their disappearance. It has several hundred members.

PROBLEMS

The activities surrounding the poultry hobby create several problems for both the hobbyist and the commercial poultryman. Many of the hobbyists are relative newcomers and do not recognize diseases and treat them with proper respect and concern. The exhibition birds are frequently exposed to contact with birds from other flocks. Many fanciers often purchase, trade or loan individual birds. This exposes a bird to disease and also creates the stress of relocation. Showing, long-distance transport, and repeated handling, may also be stresses on the birds, especially if they are not conditioned for it. Some persons who are really enthusiastic about showing may have their birds in 15 or more shows a year.

Hobbyists frequently are carried away by enthusiasm and acquire or raise too many birds for their facilities. Overcrowding, and the combining of various ages and temperaments, leads to picking and fighting in the flock. As a remedy, additional pens are hurriedly improvised which frequently prove to be unsightly and hard to clean. They are not rodent- and predator-proof and get the hobbyist in trouble with his neighbors.

There is a considerable amount of visiting back and forth among hobbists, often over long distances or on the way to or from a show. Such traffic in and out of the poultry quarters adds greatly to the possibility of exposure to disease. However, chickens are remarkably adaptable and are inherently very healthy, so the incidence of uncontrolled disease outbreaks as a result of showing is very low. But the potential for the spread of disease is real. The fact that hobby flocks can be sources of disease for the commercial industry should not be ignored.

PREVAILING PRICES

Exhibition or fancy chickens sell for a wide range of prices, depending on the quality of the individual, its source (pedigree), and the rarity of its particular kind.

Prospective breeding birds are often purchased from particular flocks because of their pedigree or because of the success of the flock's owner, even though the individuals being traded are not good candidates for the show pen. Beginners should be warned that price alone does not always indicate quality. It is a good plan to deal only with an established local breeder (whom you will see frequently) or to ask for the assistance of a respected fancier in selecting possible purchases.

PUBLICATIONS

The leading periodical serving the fancy poultry interest is *Poultry Press*. A monthly tabloid-size magazine, it is published at York, Pennsylvania by Robert DeLancey, the third-generation representative of the family that founded the magazine in 1914. It carries announcements of show, general news, management information, and a considerable amount of classified advertising.

Many of the poultry clubs issue a monthly or quarterly newsletter to generate esprit de corps, to dispense organizational information, and to develop unity of purpose. Newsletters frequently carry ads from the members of the organization. The better ones also contain timely suggestions on the management of poultry.

The American Bantam Association sends to its members a periodic letter that has an organized sequence of lessons on conditioning, growing, mating, etc., written by recognized authorities. It also issues a yearbook which lists members and official judges, and contains articles on the development of certain breeds, considerations in management, as well as a large amount of breeder advertising. Many clubs publish a directory annually. The A.P.A. has done so from time to time. In recent years one of the better ones has come from the S.P.P.A.

Many state extension services issue publications dealing with the breeding and management of poultry, much of which is applicable to exhibition poultry. Some states publish bulletins specifically for exhibition poultry raisers. Many are centered around the 4-H club programs but apply equally to interested adults.

EXHIBITION POULTRY DEFINITIONS

Breed. A group of birds having in common a given set of physical features such as type or shape, skin color, station or carriage, weight, number of toes, etc.

Variety. Subdivision of a breed usually set apart by a single factor such as color or comb type.

Classification. A group of breeds that originated or were developed in the same geographic area or country.

Disqualification. A physical defect or deformity so severe as to seriously hinder the bird's ability to perform or one which would not be desirable to transmit to future generations. The presence of any disqualification eliminates a bird from competition.

Defects. Slight departures from the desired color, shape or physical dimension. Presence of one or more defects downgrades a bird but does not eliminate it from competition.

Bantams. True-breeding miniature chickens. They exist in every breed and variety of their larger counterparts. Some forms exist as bantams only. In general, their characteristics are the same as the normal chickens whose names they carry. They are about one-fifth the size of the large fowl and often have a haughty nature and spritely manner.

A.P.A. American Poultry Association.

A.B.A. American Bantam Association.

S.P.P.A. Society for the Preservation of Poultry Antiquities.

Index

A CATALOG OF SELECTED
DOVER BOOKS
IN ALL FIELDS OF INTEREST

A CATALOG OF SELECTED DOVER
BOOKS IN ALL FIELDS OF INTEREST

CONCERNING THE SPIRITUAL IN ART, Wassily Kandinsky. Pioneering work by father of abstract art. Thoughts on color theory, nature of art. Analysis of earlier masters. 12 illustrations. 80pp. of text. 5⅜ x 8½.   23411-8 Pa. $4.95

ANIMALS: 1,419 Copyright-Free Illustrations of Mammals, Birds, Fish, Insects, etc., Jim Harter (ed.). Clear wood engravings present, in extremely lifelike poses, over 1,000 species of animals. One of the most extensive pictorial sourcebooks of its kind. Captions. Index. 284pp. 9 x 12.   23766-4 Pa. $14.95

CELTIC ART: The Methods of Construction, George Bain. Simple geometric techniques for making Celtic interlacements, spirals, Kells-type initials, animals, humans, etc. Over 500 illustrations. 160pp. 9 x 12. (Available in U.S. only.)   22923-8 Pa. $9.95

AN ATLAS OF ANATOMY FOR ARTISTS, Fritz Schider. Most thorough reference work on art anatomy in the world. Hundreds of illustrations, including selections from works by Vesalius, Leonardo, Goya, Ingres, Michelangelo, others. 593 illustrations. 192pp. 7⅛ x 10¼.   20241-0 Pa. $9.95

CELTIC HAND STROKE-BY-STROKE (Irish Half-Uncial from "The Book of Kells"): An Arthur Baker Calligraphy Manual, Arthur Baker. Complete guide to creating each letter of the alphabet in distinctive Celtic manner. Covers hand position, strokes, pens, inks, paper, more. Illustrated. 48pp. 8¼ x 11.   24336-2 Pa. $3.95

EASY ORIGAMI, John Montroll. Charming collection of 32 projects (hat, cup, pelican, piano, swan, many more) specially designed for the novice origami hobbyist. Clearly illustrated easy-to-follow instructions insure that even beginning papercrafters will achieve successful results. 48pp. 8¼ x 11.   27298-2 Pa. $3.50

THE COMPLETE BOOK OF BIRDHOUSE CONSTRUCTION FOR WOOD-WORKERS, Scott D. Campbell. Detailed instructions, illustrations, tables. Also data on bird habitat and instinct patterns. Bibliography. 3 tables. 63 illustrations in 15 figures. 48pp. 5¼ x 8½.   24407-5 Pa. $2.50

BLOOMINGDALE'S ILLUSTRATED 1886 CATALOG: Fashions, Dry Goods and Housewares, Bloomingdale Brothers. Famed merchants' extremely rare catalog depicting about 1,700 products: clothing, housewares, firearms, dry goods, jewelry, more. Invaluable for dating, identifying vintage items. Also, copyright-free graphics for artists, designers. Co-published with Henry Ford Museum & Greenfield Village. 160pp. 8¼ x 11.   25780-0 Pa. $12.95

HISTORIC COSTUME IN PICTURES, Braun & Schneider. Over 1,450 costumed figures in clearly detailed engravings—from dawn of civilization to end of 19th century. Captions. Many folk costumes. 256pp. 8⅜ x 11¾.   23150-X Pa. $12.95

CATALOG OF DOVER BOOKS

STICKLEY CRAFTSMAN FURNITURE CATALOGS, Gustav Stickley and L. & J. G. Stickley. Beautiful, functional furniture in two authentic catalogs from 1910. 594 illustrations, including 277 photos, show settles, rockers, armchairs, reclining chairs, bookcases, desks, tables. 183pp. 6½ x 9¼. 23838-5 Pa. $11.95

AMERICAN LOCOMOTIVES IN HISTORIC PHOTOGRAPHS: 1858 to 1949, Ron Ziel (ed.). A rare collection of 126 meticulously detailed official photographs, called "builder portraits," of American locomotives that majestically chronicle the rise of steam locomotive power in America. Introduction. Detailed captions. xi+ 129pp. 9 x 12. 27393-8 Pa. $13.95

AMERICA'S LIGHTHOUSES: An Illustrated History, Francis Ross Holland, Jr. Delightfully written, profusely illustrated fact-filled survey of over 200 American lighthouses since 1716. History, anecdotes, technological advances, more. 240pp. 8 x 10¾. 25576-X Pa. $12.95

TOWARDS A NEW ARCHITECTURE, Le Corbusier. Pioneering manifesto by founder of "International School." Technical and aesthetic theories, views of industry, economics, relation of form to function, "mass-production split" and much more. Profusely illustrated. 320pp. 6⅛ x 9¼. (Available in U.S. only.) 25023-7 Pa. $10.95

HOW THE OTHER HALF LIVES, Jacob Riis. Famous journalistic record, exposing poverty and degradation of New York slums around 1900, by major social reformer. 100 striking and influential photographs. 233pp. 10 x 7⅞. 22012-5 Pa. $11.95

FRUIT KEY AND TWIG KEY TO TREES AND SHRUBS, William M. Harlow. One of the handiest and most widely used identification aids. Fruit key covers 120 deciduous and evergreen species; twig key 160 deciduous species. Easily used. Over 300 photographs. 126pp. 5⅜ x 8½. 20511-8 Pa. $3.95

COMMON BIRD SONGS, Dr. Donald J. Borror. Songs of 60 most common U.S. birds: robins, sparrows, cardinals, bluejays, finches, more–arranged in order of increasing complexity. Up to 9 variations of songs of each species. Cassette and manual 99911-4 $8.95

ORCHIDS AS HOUSE PLANTS, Rebecca Tyson Northen. Grow cattleyas and many other kinds of orchids–in a window, in a case, or under artificial light. 63 illustrations. 148pp. 5⅜ x 8½. 23261-1 Pa. $7.95

MONSTER MAZES, Dave Phillips. Masterful mazes at four levels of difficulty. Avoid deadly perils and evil creatures to find magical treasures. Solutions for all 32 exciting illustrated puzzles. 48pp. 8¼ x 11. 26005-4 Pa. $2.95

MOZART'S DON GIOVANNI (DOVER OPERA LIBRETTO SERIES), Wolfgang Amadeus Mozart. Introduced and translated by Ellen H. Bleiler. Standard Italian libretto, with complete English translation. Convenient and thoroughly portable–an ideal companion for reading along with a recording or the performance itself. Introduction. List of characters. Plot summary. 121pp. 5¼ x 8½. 24944-1 Pa. $3.95

TECHNICAL MANUAL AND DICTIONARY OF CLASSICAL BALLET, Gail Grant. Defines, explains, comments on steps, movements, poses and concepts. 15-page pictorial section. Basic book for student, viewer. 127pp. 5⅜ x 8½. 21843-0 Pa. $4.95

THE CLARINET AND CLARINET PLAYING, David Pino. Lively, comprehensive work features suggestions about technique, musicianship, and musical interpretation, as well as guidelines for teaching, making your own reeds, and preparing for public performance. Includes an intriguing look at clarinet history. "A godsend," *The Clarinet,* Journal of the International Clarinet Society. Appendixes. 7 illus. 320pp. 5⅜ x 8½. 40270-3 Pa. $9.95

HOLLYWOOD GLAMOR PORTRAITS, John Kobal (ed.). 145 photos from 1926-49. Harlow, Gable, Bogart, Bacall; 94 stars in all. Full background on photographers, technical aspects. 160pp. 8⅜ x 11¼. 23352-9 Pa. $12.95

THE ANNOTATED CASEY AT THE BAT: A Collection of Ballads about the Mighty Casey/Third, Revised Edition, Martin Gardner (ed.). Amusing sequels and parodies of one of America's best-loved poems: Casey's Revenge, Why Casey Whiffed, Casey's Sister at the Bat, others. 256pp. 5⅜ x 8½. 28598-7 Pa. $8.95

THE RAVEN AND OTHER FAVORITE POEMS, Edgar Allan Poe. Over 40 of the author's most memorable poems: "The Bells," "Ulalume," "Israfel," "To Helen," "The Conqueror Worm," "Eldorado," "Annabel Lee," many more. Alphabetic lists of titles and first lines. 64pp. 5 3/16 x 8¼. 26685-0 Pa. $1.00

PERSONAL MEMOIRS OF U. S. GRANT, Ulysses Simpson Grant. Intelligent, deeply moving firsthand account of Civil War campaigns, considered by many the finest military memoirs ever written. Includes letters, historic photographs, maps and more. 528pp. 6⅛ x 9¼. 28587-1 Pa. $12.95

ANCIENT EGYPTIAN MATERIALS AND INDUSTRIES, A. Lucas and J. Harris. Fascinating, comprehensive, thoroughly documented text describes this ancient civilization's vast resources and the processes that incorporated them in daily life, including the use of animal products, building materials, cosmetics, perfumes and incense, fibers, glazed ware, glass and its manufacture, materials used in the mummification process, and much more. 544pp. 6⅛ x 9¼. (Available in U.S. only.) 40446-3 Pa. $16.95

RUSSIAN STORIES/PYCCKNE PACCKA3bl: A Dual-Language Book, edited by Gleb Struve. Twelve tales by such masters as Chekhov, Tolstoy, Dostoevsky, Pushkin, others. Excellent word-for-word English translations on facing pages, plus teaching and study aids, Russian/English vocabulary, biographical/critical introductions, more. 416pp. 5⅜ x 8½. 26244-8 Pa. $9.95

PHILADELPHIA THEN AND NOW: 60 Sites Photographed in the Past and Present, Kenneth Finkel and Susan Oyama. Rare photographs of City Hall, Logan Square, Independence Hall, Betsy Ross House, other landmarks juxtaposed with contemporary views. Captures changing face of historic city. Introduction. Captions. 128pp. 8¼ x 11. 25790-8 Pa. $9.95

AIA ARCHITECTURAL GUIDE TO NASSAU AND SUFFOLK COUNTIES, LONG ISLAND, The American Institute of Architects, Long Island Chapter, and the Society for the Preservation of Long Island Antiquities. Comprehensive, well-researched and generously illustrated volume brings to life over three centuries of Long Island's great architectural heritage. More than 240 photographs with authoritative, extensively detailed captions. 176pp. 8¼ x 11. 26946-9 Pa. $14.95

NORTH AMERICAN INDIAN LIFE: Customs and Traditions of 23 Tribes, Elsie Clews Parsons (ed.). 27 fictionalized essays by noted anthropologists examine religion, customs, government, additional facets of life among the Winnebago, Crow, Zuni, Eskimo, other tribes. 480pp. 6⅛ x 9¼. 27377-6 Pa. $10.95

FRANK LLOYD WRIGHT'S DANA HOUSE, Donald Hoffmann. Pictorial essay of residential masterpiece with over 160 interior and exterior photos, plans, elevations, sketches and studies. 128pp. 9¼ x 10¾. 29120-0 Pa. $14.95

THE MALE AND FEMALE FIGURE IN MOTION: 60 Classic Photographic Sequences, Eadweard Muybridge. 60 true-action photographs of men and women walking, running, climbing, bending, turning, etc., reproduced from rare 19th-century masterpiece. vi + 121pp. 9 x 12. 24745-7 Pa. $12.95

1001 QUESTIONS ANSWERED ABOUT THE SEASHORE, N. J. Berrill and Jacquelyn Berrill. Queries answered about dolphins, sea snails, sponges, starfish, fishes, shore birds, many others. Covers appearance, breeding, growth, feeding, much more. 305pp. 5¼ x 8¼. 23366-9 Pa. $9.95

ATTRACTING BIRDS TO YOUR YARD, William J. Weber. Easy-to-follow guide offers advice on how to attract the greatest diversity of birds: birdhouses, feeders, water and waterers, much more. 96pp. 5³⁄₁₆ x 8¼. 28927-3 Pa. $2.50

MEDICINAL AND OTHER USES OF NORTH AMERICAN PLANTS: A Historical Survey with Special Reference to the Eastern Indian Tribes, Charlotte Erichsen-Brown. Chronological historical citations document 500 years of usage of plants, trees, shrubs native to eastern Canada, northeastern U.S. Also complete identifying information. 343 illustrations. 544pp. 6½ x 9¼. 25951-X Pa. $12.95

STORYBOOK MAZES, Dave Phillips. 23 stories and mazes on two-page spreads: Wizard of Oz, Treasure Island, Robin Hood, etc. Solutions. 64pp. 8¼ x 11. 23628-5 Pa. $2.95

AMERICAN NEGRO SONGS: 230 Folk Songs and Spirituals, Religious and Secular, John W. Work. This authoritative study traces the African influences of songs sung and played by black Americans at work, in church, and as entertainment. The author discusses the lyric significance of such songs as "Swing Low, Sweet Chariot," "John Henry," and others and offers the words and music for 230 songs. Bibliography. Index of Song Titles. 272pp. 6½ x 9¼. 40271-1 Pa. $10.95

MOVIE-STAR PORTRAITS OF THE FORTIES, John Kobal (ed.). 163 glamor, studio photos of 106 stars of the 1940s: Rita Hayworth, Ava Gardner, Marlon Brando, Clark Gable, many more. 176pp. 8⅜ x 11¼. 23546-7 Pa. $14.95

BENCHLEY LOST AND FOUND, Robert Benchley. Finest humor from early 30s, about pet peeves, child psychologists, post office and others. Mostly unavailable elsewhere. 73 illustrations by Peter Arno and others. 183pp. 5⅜ x 8½. 22410-4 Pa. $6.95

YEKL and THE IMPORTED BRIDEGROOM AND OTHER STORIES OF YIDDISH NEW YORK, Abraham Cahan. Film Hester Street based on *Yekl* (1896). Novel, other stories among first about Jewish immigrants on N.Y.'s East Side. 240pp. 5⅜ x 8½. 22427-9 Pa. $7.95

SELECTED POEMS, Walt Whitman. Generous sampling from *Leaves of Grass*. Twenty-four poems include "I Hear America Singing," "Song of the Open Road," "I Sing the Body Electric," "When Lilacs Last in the Dooryard Bloom'd," "O Captain! My Captain!"–all reprinted from an authoritative edition. Lists of titles and first lines. 128pp. 5³⁄₁₆ x 8¼. 26878-0 Pa. $1.00

THE BEST TALES OF HOFFMANN, E. T. A. Hoffmann. 10 of Hoffmann's most important stories: "Nutcracker and the King of Mice," "The Golden Flowerpot," etc. 458pp. 5⅜ x 8½. 21793-0 Pa. $9.95

FROM FETISH TO GOD IN ANCIENT EGYPT, E. A. Wallis Budge. Rich detailed survey of Egyptian conception of "God" and gods, magic, cult of animals, Osiris, more. Also, superb English translations of hymns and legends. 240 illustrations. 545pp. 5⅜ x 8½. 25803-3 Pa. $13.95

FRENCH STORIES/CONTES FRANÇAIS: A Dual-Language Book, Wallace Fowlie. Ten stories by French masters, Voltaire to Camus: "Micromegas" by Voltaire; "The Atheist's Mass" by Balzac; "Minuet" by de Maupassant; "The Guest" by Camus, six more. Excellent English translations on facing pages. Also French-English vocabulary list, exercises, more. 352pp. 5⅜ x 8½. 26443-2 Pa. $9.95

CHICAGO AT THE TURN OF THE CENTURY IN PHOTOGRAPHS: 122 Historic Views from the Collections of the Chicago Historical Society, Larry A. Viskochil. Rare large-format prints offer detailed views of City Hall, State Street, the Loop, Hull House, Union Station, many other landmarks, circa 1904-1913. Introduction. Captions. Maps. 144pp. 9⅜ x 12¼. 24656-6 Pa. $12.95

OLD BROOKLYN IN EARLY PHOTOGRAPHS, 1865-1929, William Lee Younger. Luna Park, Gravesend race track, construction of Grand Army Plaza, moving of Hotel Brighton, etc. 157 previously unpublished photographs. 165pp. 8⅞ x 11¾. 23587-4 Pa. $13.95

THE MYTHS OF THE NORTH AMERICAN INDIANS, Lewis Spence. Rich anthology of the myths and legends of the Algonquins, Iroquois, Pawnees and Sioux, prefaced by an extensive historical and ethnological commentary. 36 illustrations. 480pp. 5⅜ x 8½. 25967-6 Pa. $10.95

AN ENCYCLOPEDIA OF BATTLES: Accounts of Over 1,560 Battles from 1479 B.C. to the Present, David Eggenberger. Essential details of every major battle in recorded history from the first battle of Megiddo in 1479 B.C. to Grenada in 1984. List of Battle Maps. New Appendix covering the years 1967-1984. Index. 99 illustrations. 544pp. 6½ x 9¼. 24913-1 Pa. $16.95

SAILING ALONE AROUND THE WORLD, Captain Joshua Slocum. First man to sail around the world, alone, in small boat. One of great feats of seamanship told in delightful manner. 67 illustrations. 294pp. 5⅜ x 8½. 20326-3 Pa. $6.95

ANARCHISM AND OTHER ESSAYS, Emma Goldman. Powerful, penetrating, prophetic essays on direct action, role of minorities, prison reform, puritan hypocrisy, violence, etc. 271pp. 5⅜ x 8½. 22484-8 Pa. $8.95

MYTHS OF THE HINDUS AND BUDDHISTS, Ananda K. Coomaraswamy and Sister Nivedita. Great stories of the epics; deeds of Krishna, Shiva, taken from puranas, Vedas, folk tales; etc. 32 illustrations. 400pp. 5⅜ x 8½. 21759-0 Pa. $12.95

THE TRAUMA OF BIRTH, Otto Rank. Rank's controversial thesis that anxiety neurosis is caused by profound psychological trauma which occurs at birth. 256pp. 5⅜ x 8½. 27974-X Pa. $7.95

A THEOLOGICO-POLITICAL TREATISE, Benedict Spinoza. Also contains unfinished Political Treatise. Great classic on religious liberty, theory of government on common consent. R. Elwes translation. Total of 421pp. 5⅜ x 8½. 20249-6 Pa. $10.95

MY BONDAGE AND MY FREEDOM, Frederick Douglass. Born a slave, Douglass became outspoken force in antislavery movement. The best of Douglass' autobiographies. Graphic description of slave life. 464pp. 5⅜ x 8½. 22457-0 Pa. $8.95

FOLLOWING THE EQUATOR: A Journey Around the World, Mark Twain. Fascinating humorous account of 1897 voyage to Hawaii, Australia, India, New Zealand, etc. Ironic, bemused reports on peoples, customs, climate, flora and fauna, politics, much more. 197 illustrations. 720pp. 5⅜ x 8½. 26113-1 Pa. $15.95

THE PEOPLE CALLED SHAKERS, Edward D. Andrews. Definitive study of Shakers: origins, beliefs, practices, dances, social organization, furniture and crafts, etc. 33 illustrations. 351pp. 5⅜ x 8½. 21081-2 Pa. $12.95

THE MYTHS OF GREECE AND ROME, H. A. Guerber. A classic of mythology, generously illustrated, long prized for its simple, graphic, accurate retelling of the principal myths of Greece and Rome, and for its commentary on their origins and significance. With 64 illustrations by Michelangelo, Raphael, Titian, Rubens, Canova, Bernini and others. 480pp. 5⅜ x 8½. 27584-1 Pa. $10.95

PSYCHOLOGY OF MUSIC, Carl E. Seashore. Classic work discusses music as a medium from psychological viewpoint. Clear treatment of physical acoustics, auditory apparatus, sound perception, development of musical skills, nature of musical feeling, host of other topics. 88 figures. 408pp. 5⅜ x 8½. 21851-1 Pa. $11.95

THE PHILOSOPHY OF HISTORY, Georg W. Hegel. Great classic of Western thought develops concept that history is not chance but rational process, the evolution of freedom. 457pp. 5⅜ x 8½. 20112-0 Pa. $9.95

THE BOOK OF TEA, Kakuzo Okakura. Minor classic of the Orient: entertaining, charming explanation, interpretation of traditional Japanese culture in terms of tea ceremony. 94pp. 5⅜ x 8½. 20070-1 Pa. $3.95

LIFE IN ANCIENT EGYPT, Adolf Erman. Fullest, most thorough, detailed older account with much not in more recent books, domestic life, religion, magic, medicine, commerce, much more. Many illustrations reproduce tomb paintings, carvings, hieroglyphs, etc. 597pp. 5⅜ x 8½. 22632-8 Pa. $12.95

SUNDIALS, Their Theory and Construction, Albert Waugh. Far and away the best, most thorough coverage of ideas, mathematics concerned, types, construction, adjusting anywhere. Simple, nontechnical treatment allows even children to build several of these dials. Over 100 illustrations. 230pp. 5⅜ x 8½. 22947-5 Pa. $8.95

THEORETICAL HYDRODYNAMICS, L. M. Milne Thomson. Classic exposition of the mathematical theory of fluid motion, applicable to both hydrodynamics and aerodynamics. Over 600 exercises. 768pp. 6⅛ x 9¼. 68970-0 Pa. $20.95

SONGS OF EXPERIENCE: Facsimile Reproduction with 26 Plates in Full Color, William Blake. 26 full-color plates from a rare 1826 edition. Includes "TheTyger," "London," "Holy Thursday," and other poems. Printed text of poems. 48pp. 5¼ x 7. 24636-1 Pa. $4.95

OLD-TIME VIGNETTES IN FULL COLOR, Carol Belanger Grafton (ed.). Over 390 charming, often sentimental illustrations, selected from archives of Victorian graphics—pretty women posing, children playing, food, flowers, kittens and puppies, smiling cherubs, birds and butterflies, much more. All copyright-free. 48pp. 9¼ x 12¼. 27269-9 Pa. $9.95

PERSPECTIVE FOR ARTISTS, Rex Vicat Cole. Depth, perspective of sky and sea, shadows, much more, not usually covered. 391 diagrams, 81 reproductions of drawings and paintings. 279pp. 5⅜ x 8½. 22487-2 Pa. $9.95

DRAWING THE LIVING FIGURE, Joseph Sheppard. Innovative approach to artistic anatomy focuses on specifics of surface anatomy, rather than muscles and bones. Over 170 drawings of live models in front, back and side views, and in widely varying poses. Accompanying diagrams. 177 illustrations. Introduction. Index. 144pp. 8⅜ x11¼. 26723-7 Pa. $9.95

GOTHIC AND OLD ENGLISH ALPHABETS: 100 Complete Fonts, Dan X. Solo. Add power, elegance to posters, signs, other graphics with 100 stunning copyright-free alphabets: Blackstone, Dolbey, Germania, 97 more–including many lower-case, numerals, punctuation marks. 104pp. 8⅛ x 11. 24695-7 Pa. $9.95

HOW TO DO BEADWORK, Mary White. Fundamental book on craft from simple projects to five-bead chains and woven works. 106 illustrations. 142pp. 5⅜ x 8. 20697-1 Pa. $5.95

THE BOOK OF WOOD CARVING, Charles Marshall Sayers. Finest book for beginners discusses fundamentals and offers 34 designs. "Absolutely first rate . . . well thought out and well executed."–E. J. Tangerman. 118pp. 7¾ x 10⅝. 23654-4 Pa. $7.95

ILLUSTRATED CATALOG OF CIVIL WAR MILITARY GOODS: Union Army Weapons, Insignia, Uniform Accessories, and Other Equipment, Schuyler, Hartley, and Graham. Rare, profusely illustrated 1846 catalog includes Union Army uniform and dress regulations, arms and ammunition, coats, insignia, flags, swords, rifles, etc. 226 illustrations. 160pp. 9 x 12. 24939-5 Pa. $12.95

WOMEN'S FASHIONS OF THE EARLY 1900s: An Unabridged Republication of "New York Fashions, 1909," National Cloak & Suit Co. Rare catalog of mail-order fashions documents women's and children's clothing styles shortly after the turn of the century. Captions offer full descriptions, prices. Invaluable resource for fashion, costume historians. Approximately 725 illustrations. 128pp. 8⅜ x 11¼. 27276-1 Pa. $12.95

THE 1912 AND 1915 GUSTAV STICKLEY FURNITURE CATALOGS, Gustav Stickley. With over 200 detailed illustrations and descriptions, these two catalogs are essential reading and reference materials and identification guides for Stickley furniture. Captions cite materials, dimensions and prices. 112pp. 6½ x 9¼. 26676-1 Pa. $9.95

EARLY AMERICAN LOCOMOTIVES, John H. White, Jr. Finest locomotive engravings from early 19th century: historical (1804–74), main-line (after 1870), special, foreign, etc. 147 plates. 142pp. 11⅜ x 8¼. 22772-3 Pa. $12.95

THE TALL SHIPS OF TODAY IN PHOTOGRAPHS, Frank O. Braynard. Lavishly illustrated tribute to nearly 100 majestic contemporary sailing vessels: Amerigo Vespucci, Clearwater, Constitution, Eagle, Mayflower, Sea Cloud, Victory, many more. Authoritative captions provide statistics, background on each ship. 190 black-and-white photographs and illustrations. Introduction. 128pp. 8⅞ x 11¾. 27163-3 Pa. $14.95

LITTLE BOOK OF EARLY AMERICAN CRAFTS AND TRADES, Peter Stockham (ed.). 1807 children's book explains crafts and trades: baker, hatter, cooper, potter, and many others. 23 copperplate illustrations. 140pp. 4⅝ x 6.
23336-7 Pa. $4.95

VICTORIAN FASHIONS AND COSTUMES FROM HARPER'S BAZAR, 1867–1898, Stella Blum (ed.). Day costumes, evening wear, sports clothes, shoes, hats, other accessories in over 1,000 detailed engravings. 320pp. 9⅜ x 12¼.
22990-4 Pa. $16.95

GUSTAV STICKLEY, THE CRAFTSMAN, Mary Ann Smith. Superb study surveys broad scope of Stickley's achievement, especially in architecture. Design philosophy, rise and fall of the Craftsman empire, descriptions and floor plans for many Craftsman houses, more. 86 black-and-white halftones. 31 line illustrations. Introduction 208pp. 6½ x 9¼.
27210-9 Pa. $9.95

THE LONG ISLAND RAIL ROAD IN EARLY PHOTOGRAPHS, Ron Ziel. Over 220 rare photos, informative text document origin (1844) and development of rail service on Long Island. Vintage views of early trains, locomotives, stations, passengers, crews, much more. Captions. 8⅞ x 11¾.
26301-0 Pa. $14.95

VOYAGE OF THE LIBERDADE, Joshua Slocum. Great 19th-century mariner's thrilling, first-hand account of the wreck of his ship off South America, the 35-foot boat he built from the wreckage, and its remarkable voyage home. 128pp. 5⅜ x 8½.
40022-0 Pa. $5.95

TEN BOOKS ON ARCHITECTURE, Vitruvius. The most important book ever written on architecture. Early Roman aesthetics, technology, classical orders, site selection, all other aspects. Morgan translation. 331pp. 5⅜ x 8½. 20645-9 Pa. $9.95

THE HUMAN FIGURE IN MOTION, Eadweard Muybridge. More than 4,500 stopped-action photos, in action series, showing undraped men, women, children jumping, lying down, throwing, sitting, wrestling, carrying, etc. 390pp. 7⅞ x 10⅝.
20204-6 Clothbd. $29.95

TREES OF THE EASTERN AND CENTRAL UNITED STATES AND CANADA, William M. Harlow. Best one-volume guide to 140 trees. Full descriptions, woodlore, range, etc. Over 600 illustrations. Handy size. 288pp. 4½ x 6⅜.
20395-6 Pa. $6.95

SONGS OF WESTERN BIRDS, Dr. Donald J. Borror. Complete song and call repertoire of 60 western species, including flycatchers, juncoes, cactus wrens, many more–includes fully illustrated booklet. Cassette and manual 99913-0 $8.95

GROWING AND USING HERBS AND SPICES, Milo Miloradovich. Versatile handbook provides all the information needed for cultivation and use of all the herbs and spices available in North America. 4 illustrations. Index. Glossary. 236pp. 5⅜ x 8½.
25058-X Pa. $7.95

BIG BOOK OF MAZES AND LABYRINTHS, Walter Shepherd. 50 mazes and labyrinths in all–classical, solid, ripple, and more–in one great volume. Perfect inexpensive puzzler for clever youngsters. Full solutions. 112pp. 8⅛ x 11.
22951-3 Pa. $5.95

PIANO TUNING, J. Cree Fischer. Clearest, best book for beginner, amateur. Simple repairs, raising dropped notes, tuning by easy method of flattened fifths. No previous skills needed. 4 illustrations. 201pp. 5⅜ x 8½. 23267-0 Pa. $6.95

HINTS TO SINGERS, Lillian Nordica. Selecting the right teacher, developing confidence, overcoming stage fright, and many other important skills receive thoughtful discussion in this indispensible guide, written by a world-famous diva of four decades' experience. 96pp. 5⅜ x 8½. 40094-8 Pa. $4.95

THE COMPLETE NONSENSE OF EDWARD LEAR, Edward Lear. All nonsense limericks, zany alphabets, Owl and Pussycat, songs, nonsense botany, etc., illustrated by Lear. Total of 320pp. 5⅜ x 8½. (Available in U.S. only.) 20167-8 Pa. $7.95

VICTORIAN PARLOUR POETRY: An Annotated Anthology, Michael R. Turner. 117 gems by Longfellow, Tennyson, Browning, many lesser-known poets. "The Village Blacksmith," "Curfew Must Not Ring Tonight," "Only a Baby Small," dozens more, often difficult to find elsewhere. Index of poets, titles, first lines. xxiii + 325pp. 5⅝ x 8¼. 27044-0 Pa. $12.95

DUBLINERS, James Joyce. Fifteen stories offer vivid, tightly focused observations of the lives of Dublin's poorer classes. At least one, "The Dead," is considered a masterpiece. Reprinted complete and unabridged from standard edition. 160pp. 5 3/16 x 8¼. 26870-5 Pa. $1.50

GREAT WEIRD TALES: 14 Stories by Lovecraft, Blackwood, Machen and Others, S. T. Joshi (ed.). 14 spellbinding tales, including "The Sin Eater," by Fiona McLeod, "The Eye Above the Mantel," by Frank Belknap Long, as well as renowned works by R. H. Barlow, Lord Dunsany, Arthur Machen, W. C. Morrow and eight other masters of the genre. 256pp. 5⅜ x 8½. (Available in U.S. only.) 40436-6 Pa. $8.95

THE BOOK OF THE SACRED MAGIC OF ABRAMELIN THE MAGE, translated by S. MacGregor Mathers. Medieval manuscript of ceremonial magic. Basic document in Aleister Crowley, Golden Dawn groups. 268pp. 5⅜ x 8½. 23211-5 Pa. $9.95

NEW RUSSIAN-ENGLISH AND ENGLISH-RUSSIAN DICTIONARY, M. A. O'Brien. This is a remarkably handy Russian dictionary, containing a surprising amount of information, including over 70,000 entries. 366pp. 4½ x 6⅛. 20208-9 Pa. $10.95

HISTORIC HOMES OF THE AMERICAN PRESIDENTS, Second, Revised Edition, Irvin Haas. A traveler's guide to American Presidential homes, most open to the public, depicting and describing homes occupied by every American President from George Washington to George Bush. With visiting hours, admission charges, travel routes. 175 photographs. Index. 160pp. 8¼ x 11. 26751-2 Pa. $13.95

NEW YORK IN THE FORTIES, Andreas Feininger. 162 brilliant photographs by the well-known photographer, formerly with *Life* magazine. Commuters, shoppers, Times Square at night, much else from city at its peak. Captions by John von Hartz. 181pp. 9¼ x 10¾. 23585-8 Pa. $13.95

INDIAN SIGN LANGUAGE, William Tomkins. Over 525 signs developed by Sioux and other tribes. Written instructions and diagrams. Also 290 pictographs. 111pp. 6⅛ x 9¼. 22029-X Pa. $3.95

ANATOMY: A Complete Guide for Artists, Joseph Sheppard. A master of figure drawing shows artists how to render human anatomy convincingly. Over 460 illustrations. 224pp. 8⅜ x 11¼. 27279-6 Pa. $11.95

MEDIEVAL CALLIGRAPHY: Its History and Technique, Marc Drogin. Spirited history, comprehensive instruction manual covers 13 styles (ca. 4th century through 15th). Excellent photographs; directions for duplicating medieval techniques with modern tools. 224pp. 8⅜ x 11¼. 26142-5 Pa. $12.95

DRIED FLOWERS: How to Prepare Them, Sarah Whitlock and Martha Rankin. Complete instructions on how to use silica gel, meal and borax, perlite aggregate, sand and borax, glycerine and water to create attractive permanent flower arrangements. 12 illustrations. 32pp. 5⅜ x 8½. 21802-3 Pa. $1.00

EASY-TO-MAKE BIRD FEEDERS FOR WOODWORKERS, Scott D. Campbell. Detailed, simple-to-use guide for designing, constructing, caring for and using feeders. Text, illustrations for 12 classic and contemporary designs. 96pp. 5⅜ x 8½. 25847-5 Pa. $3.95

SCOTTISH WONDER TALES FROM MYTH AND LEGEND, Donald A. Mackenzie. 16 lively tales tell of giants rumbling down mountainsides, of a magic wand that turns stone pillars into warriors, of gods and goddesses, evil hags, powerful forces and more. 240pp. 5⅜ x 8½. 29677-6 Pa. $6.95

THE HISTORY OF UNDERCLOTHES, C. Willett Cunnington and Phyllis Cunnington. Fascinating, well-documented survey covering six centuries of English undergarments, enhanced with over 100 illustrations: 12th-century laced-up bodice, footed long drawers (1795), 19th-century bustles, 19th-century corsets for men, Victorian "bust improvers," much more. 272pp. 5⅝ x 8¼. 27124-2 Pa. $9.95

ARTS AND CRAFTS FURNITURE: The Complete Brooks Catalog of 1912, Brooks Manufacturing Co. Photos and detailed descriptions of more than 150 now very collectible furniture designs from the Arts and Crafts movement depict davenports, settees, buffets, desks, tables, chairs, bedsteads, dressers and more, all built of solid, quarter-sawed oak. Invaluable for students and enthusiasts of antiques, Americana and the decorative arts. 80pp. 6½ x 9¼. 27471-3 Pa. $8.95

WILBUR AND ORVILLE: A Biography of the Wright Brothers, Fred Howard. Definitive, crisply written study tells the full story of the brothers' lives and work. A vividly written biography, unparalleled in scope and color, that also captures the spirit of an extraordinary era. 560pp. 6⅛ x 9¼. 40297-5 Pa. $17.95

THE ARTS OF THE SAILOR: Knotting, Splicing and Ropework, Hervey Garrett Smith. Indispensable shipboard reference covers tools, basic knots and useful hitches; handsewing and canvas work, more. Over 100 illustrations. Delightful reading for sea lovers. 256pp. 5⅜ x 8½. 26440-8 Pa. $8.95

FRANK LLOYD WRIGHT'S FALLINGWATER: The House and Its History, Second, Revised Edition, Donald Hoffmann. A total revision–both in text and illustrations–of the standard document on Fallingwater, the boldest, most personal architectural statement of Wright's mature years, updated with valuable new material from the recently opened Frank Lloyd Wright Archives. "Fascinating"–*The New York Times*. 116 illustrations. 128pp. 9¼ x 10¾. 27430-6 Pa. $12.95

PHOTOGRAPHIC SKETCHBOOK OF THE CIVIL WAR, Alexander Gardner. 100 photos taken on field during the Civil War. Famous shots of Manassas Harper's Ferry, Lincoln, Richmond, slave pens, etc. 244pp. 10⅝ x 8¼. 22731-6 Pa. $10.95

FIVE ACRES AND INDEPENDENCE, Maurice G. Kains. Great back-to-the-land classic explains basics of self-sufficient farming. The one book to get. 95 illustrations. 397pp. 5⅜ x 8½. 20974-1 Pa. $7.95

SONGS OF EASTERN BIRDS, Dr. Donald J. Borror. Songs and calls of 60 species most common to eastern U.S.: warblers, woodpeckers, flycatchers, thrushes, larks, many more in high-quality recording. Cassette and manual 99912-2 $9.95

A MODERN HERBAL, Margaret Grieve. Much the fullest, most exact, most useful compilation of herbal material. Gigantic alphabetical encyclopedia, from aconite to zedoary, gives botanical information, medical properties, folklore, economic uses, much else. Indispensable to serious reader. 161 illustrations. 888pp. 6½ x 9¼. 2-vol. set. (Available in U.S. only.) Vol. I: 22798-7 Pa. $10.95
Vol. II: 22799-5 Pa. $10.95

HIDDEN TREASURE MAZE BOOK, Dave Phillips. Solve 34 challenging mazes accompanied by heroic tales of adventure. Evil dragons, people-eating plants, bloodthirsty giants, many more dangerous adversaries lurk at every twist and turn. 34 mazes, stories, solutions. 48pp. 8¼ x 11. 24566-7 Pa. $2.95

LETTERS OF W. A. MOZART, Wolfgang A. Mozart. Remarkable letters show bawdy wit, humor, imagination, musical insights, contemporary musical world; includes some letters from Leopold Mozart. 276pp. 5⅜ x 8½. 22859-2 Pa. $9.95

BASIC PRINCIPLES OF CLASSICAL BALLET, Agrippina Vaganova. Great Russian theoretician, teacher explains methods for teaching classical ballet. 118 illustrations. 175pp. 5⅜ x 8½. 22036-2 Pa. $6.95

THE JUMPING FROG, Mark Twain. Revenge edition. The original story of The Celebrated Jumping Frog of Calaveras County, a hapless French translation, and Twain's hilarious "retranslation" from the French. 12 illustrations. 66pp. 5⅜ x 8½. 22686-7 Pa. $4.95

BEST REMEMBERED POEMS, Martin Gardner (ed.). The 126 poems in this superb collection of 19th- and 20th-century British and American verse range from Shelley's "To a Skylark" to the impassioned "Renascence" of Edna St. Vincent Millay and to Edward Lear's whimsical "The Owl and the Pussycat." 224pp. 5⅜ x 8½. 27165-X Pa. $5.95

COMPLETE SONNETS, William Shakespeare. Over 150 exquisite poems deal with love, friendship, the tyranny of time, beauty's evanescence, death and other themes in language of remarkable power, precision and beauty. Glossary of archaic terms. 80pp. 5³⁄₁₆ x 8¼. 26686-9 Pa. $1.00

THE BATTLES THAT CHANGED HISTORY, Fletcher Pratt. Eminent historian profiles 16 crucial conflicts, ancient to modern, that changed the course of civilization. 352pp. 5⅜ x 8½. 41129-X Pa. $9.95

THE WIT AND HUMOR OF OSCAR WILDE, Alvin Redman (ed.). More than 1,000 ripostes, paradoxes, wisecracks: Work is the curse of the drinking classes; I can resist everything except temptation; etc. 258pp. 5⅜ x 8½. 20602-5 Pa. $6.95

SHAKESPEARE LEXICON AND QUOTATION DICTIONARY, Alexander Schmidt. Full definitions, locations, shades of meaning in every word in plays and poems. More than 50,000 exact quotations. 1,485pp. 6½ x 9¼. 2-vol. set.
Vol. 1: 22726-X Pa. $17.95
Vol. 2: 22727-8 Pa. $17.95

SELECTED POEMS, Emily Dickinson. Over 100 best-known, best-loved poems by one of America's foremost poets, reprinted from authoritative early editions. No comparable edition at this price. Index of first lines. 64pp. 5³⁄₁₆ x 8¼. 26466-1 Pa. $1.00

THE INSIDIOUS DR. FU-MANCHU, Sax Rohmer. The first of the popular mystery series introduces a pair of English detectives to their archnemesis, the diabolical Dr. Fu-Manchu. Flavorful atmosphere, fast-paced action, and colorful characters enliven this classic of the genre. 208pp. 5³⁄₁₆ x 8¼. 29898-1 Pa. $2.00

THE MALLEUS MALEFICARUM OF KRAMER AND SPRENGER, translated by Montague Summers. Full text of most important witchhunter's "bible," used by both Catholics and Protestants. 278pp. 6⅝ x 10. 22802-9 Pa. $12.95

SPANISH STORIES/CUENTOS ESPAÑOLES: A Dual-Language Book, Angel Flores (ed.). Unique format offers 13 great stories in Spanish by Cervantes, Borges, others. Faithful English translations on facing pages. 352pp. 5⅜ x 8½. 25399-6 Pa. $9.95

GARDEN CITY, LONG ISLAND, IN EARLY PHOTOGRAPHS, 1869–1919, Mildred H. Smith. Handsome treasury of 118 vintage pictures, accompanied by carefully researched captions, document the Garden City Hotel fire (1899), the Vanderbilt Cup Race (1908), the first airmail flight departing from the Nassau Boulevard Aerodrome (1911), and much more. 96pp. 8⅞ x 11¾. 40669-5 Pa. $12.95

OLD QUEENS, N.Y., IN EARLY PHOTOGRAPHS, Vincent F. Seyfried and William Asadorian. Over 160 rare photographs of Maspeth, Jamaica, Jackson Heights, and other areas. Vintage views of DeWitt Clinton mansion, 1939 World's Fair and more. Captions. 192pp. 8⅞ x 11. 26358-4 Pa. $14.95

CAPTURED BY THE INDIANS: 15 Firsthand Accounts, 1750-1870, Frederick Drimmer. Astounding true historical accounts of grisly torture, bloody conflicts, relentless pursuits, miraculous escapes and more, by people who lived to tell the tale. 384pp. 5⅜ x 8½. 24901-8 Pa. $9.95

THE WORLD'S GREAT SPEECHES (Fourth Enlarged Edition), Lewis Copeland, Lawrence W. Lamm, and Stephen J. McKenna. Nearly 300 speeches provide public speakers with a wealth of updated quotes and inspiration–from Pericles' funeral oration and William Jennings Bryan's "Cross of Gold Speech" to Malcolm X's powerful words on the Black Revolution and Earl of Spenser's tribute to his sister, Diana, Princess of Wales. 944pp. 5⅜ x 8⅜. 40903-1 Pa. $15.95

THE BOOK OF THE SWORD, Sir Richard F. Burton. Great Victorian scholar/adventurer's eloquent, erudite history of the "queen of weapons"–from prehistory to early Roman Empire. Evolution and development of early swords, variations (sabre, broadsword, cutlass, scimitar, etc.), much more. 336pp. 6⅛ x 9¼. 25434-8 Pa. $9.95

AUTOBIOGRAPHY: The Story of My Experiments with Truth, Mohandas K. Gandhi. Boyhood, legal studies, purification, the growth of the Satyagraha (nonviolent protest) movement. Critical, inspiring work of the man responsible for the freedom of India. 480pp. 5⅜ x 8½. (Available in U.S. only.) 24593-4 Pa. $9.95

CELTIC MYTHS AND LEGENDS, T. W. Rolleston. Masterful retelling of Irish and Welsh stories and tales. Cuchulain, King Arthur, Deirdre, the Grail, many more. First paperback edition. 58 full-page illustrations. 512pp. 5⅜ x 8½. 26507-2 Pa. $9.95

THE PRINCIPLES OF PSYCHOLOGY, William James. Famous long course complete, unabridged. Stream of thought, time perception, memory, experimental methods; great work decades ahead of its time. 94 figures. 1,391pp. 5⅜ x 8½. 2-vol. set.
Vol. I: 20381-6 Pa. $14.95
Vol. II: 20382-4 Pa. $16.95

THE WORLD AS WILL AND REPRESENTATION, Arthur Schopenhauer. Definitive English translation of Schopenhauer's life work, correcting more than 1,000 errors, omissions in earlier translations. Translated by E. F. J. Payne. Total of 1,269pp. 5⅜ x 8½. 2-vol. set. Vol. 1: 21761-2 Pa. $12.95
Vol. 2: 21762-0 Pa. $12.95

MAGIC AND MYSTERY IN TIBET, Madame Alexandra David-Neel. Experiences among lamas, magicians, sages, sorcerers, Bonpa wizards. A true psychic discovery. 32 illustrations. 321pp. 5⅜ x 8½. (Available in U.S. only.) 22682-4 Pa. $9.95

THE EGYPTIAN BOOK OF THE DEAD, E. A. Wallis Budge. Complete reproduction of Ani's papyrus, finest ever found. Full hieroglyphic text, interlinear transliteration, word-for-word translation, smooth translation. 533pp. 6½ x 9¼.
21866-X Pa. $12.95

MATHEMATICS FOR THE NONMATHEMATICIAN, Morris Kline. Detailed, college-level treatment of mathematics in cultural and historical context, with numerous exercises. Recommended Reading Lists. Tables. Numerous figures. 641pp. 5⅜ x 8½.
24823-2 Pa. $11.95

PROBABILISTIC METHODS IN THE THEORY OF STRUCTURES, Isaac Elishakoff. Well-written introduction covers the elements of the theory of probability from two or more random variables, the reliability of such multivariable structures, the theory of random function, Monte Carlo methods of treating problems incapable of exact solution, and more. Examples. 502pp. 5⅜ x 8½. 40691-1 Pa. $16.95

THE RIME OF THE ANCIENT MARINER, Gustave Doré, S. T. Coleridge. Doré's finest work; 34 plates capture moods, subtleties of poem. Flawless full-size reproductions printed on facing pages with authoritative text of poem. "Beautiful. Simply beautiful."–*Publisher's Weekly.* 77pp. 9¼ x 12. 22305-1 Pa. $7.95

NORTH AMERICAN INDIAN DESIGNS FOR ARTISTS AND CRAFTSPEOPLE, Eva Wilson. Over 360 authentic copyright-free designs adapted from Navajo blankets, Hopi pottery, Sioux buffalo hides, more. Geometrics, symbolic figures, plant and animal motifs, etc. 128pp. 8⅜ x 11. (Not for sale in the United Kingdom.) 25341-4 Pa. $9.95

SCULPTURE: Principles and Practice, Louis Slobodkin. Step-by-step approach to clay, plaster, metals, stone; classical and modern. 253 drawings, photos. 255pp. 8⅛ x 11.
22960-2 Pa. $11.95

THE INFLUENCE OF SEA POWER UPON HISTORY, 1660–1783, A. T. Mahan. Influential classic of naval history and tactics still used as text in war colleges. First paperback edition. 4 maps. 24 battle plans. 640pp. 5⅜ x 8½. 25509-3 Pa. $14.95

THE STORY OF THE TITANIC AS TOLD BY ITS SURVIVORS, Jack Winocour (ed.). What it was really like. Panic, despair, shocking inefficiency, and a little heroism. More thrilling than any fictional account. 26 illustrations. 320pp. 5⅜ x 8½. 20610-6 Pa. $8.95

FAIRY AND FOLK TALES OF THE IRISH PEASANTRY, William Butler Yeats (ed.). Treasury of 64 tales from the twilight world of Celtic myth and legend: "The Soul Cages," "The Kildare Pooka," "King O'Toole and his Goose," many more. Introduction and Notes by W. B. Yeats. 352pp. 5⅜ x 8½. 26941-8 Pa. $8.95

BUDDHIST MAHAYANA TEXTS, E. B. Cowell and others (eds.). Superb, accurate translations of basic documents in Mahayana Buddhism, highly important in history of religions. The Buddha-karita of Asvaghosha, Larger Sukhavativyuha, more. 448pp. 5⅜ x 8½. 25552-2 Pa. $12.95

ONE TWO THREE . . . INFINITY: Facts and Speculations of Science, George Gamow. Great physicist's fascinating, readable overview of contemporary science: number theory, relativity, fourth dimension, entropy, genes, atomic structure, much more. 128 illustrations. Index. 352pp. 5⅜ x 8½. 25664-2 Pa. $9.95

EXPERIMENTATION AND MEASUREMENT, W. J. Youden. Introductory manual explains laws of measurement in simple terms and offers tips for achieving accuracy and minimizing errors. Mathematics of measurement, use of instruments, experimenting with machines. 1994 edition. Foreword. Preface. Introduction. Epilogue. Selected Readings. Glossary. Index. Tables and figures. 128pp. 5³/₈ x 8¹/₂. 40451-X Pa. $6.95

DALÍ ON MODERN ART: The Cuckolds of Antiquated Modern Art, Salvador Dalí. Influential painter skewers modern art and its practitioners. Outrageous evaluations of Picasso, Cézanne, Turner, more. 15 renderings of paintings discussed. 44 calligraphic decorations by Dalí. 96pp. 5⅜ x 8½. (Available in U.S. only.) 29220-7 Pa. $5.95

ANTIQUE PLAYING CARDS: A Pictorial History, Henry René D'Allemagne. Over 900 elaborate, decorative images from rare playing cards (14th–20th centuries): Bacchus, death, dancing dogs, hunting scenes, royal coats of arms, players cheating, much more. 96pp. 9¼ x 12¼. 29265-7 Pa. $12.95

MAKING FURNITURE MASTERPIECES: 30 Projects with Measured Drawings, Franklin H. Gottshall. Step-by-step instructions, illustrations for constructing handsome, useful pieces, among them a Sheraton desk, Chippendale chair, Spanish desk, Queen Anne table and a William and Mary dressing mirror. 224pp. 8⅛ x 11¼. 29338-6 Pa. $16.95

THE FOSSIL BOOK: A Record of Prehistoric Life, Patricia V. Rich et al. Profusely illustrated definitive guide covers everything from single-celled organisms and dinosaurs to birds and mammals and the interplay between climate and man. Over 1,500 illustrations. 760pp. 7½ x 10⅛. 29371-8 Pa. $29.95

Prices subject to change without notice.

Available at your book dealer or write for free catalog to Dept. GI, Dover Publications, Inc., 31 East 2nd St., Mineola, N.Y. 11501. Dover publishes more than 500 books each year on science, elementary and advanced mathematics, biology, music, art, literary history, social sciences and other areas.